WE COUNT IT ALL JOY

Other Books by Rachel

Poetry
This is How You Know
Life: a definition of terms

Essay
Parenthood: Has Anyone Seen My Sanity?
The Life-Changing Madness of Tidying Up After Children
This Life With Boys

To see all the books Rachel has written, please click or visit the link below:

www.racheltoalson.com/writing

RACHEL TOALSON

WE
COUNT IT
ALL
JOY

BATLEE
PRESS

Batlee Press
PO Box 591596
San Antonio, TX 78259

Copyright ©2018 by Rachel Toalson
All rights reserved.

No part of this book may be reproduced or transmitted in any form or by any means, electronic or mechanical, including photocopying and recording, or by any information storage and retrieval system, without permission in writing. For information, address Batlee Press, PO Box 591596, San Antonio, TX 78259.

The author appreciates your taking the time to read her work. Please consider leaving a review wherever you bought it, or telling your friends how much you enjoyed it. Both of those help get the book into the hands of new readers, which is incredibly important for authors. Thank you for your support.
www.racheltoalson.com

Manufactured in the United States of America

First Edition—2018/Cover designed by Toalson Marketing
www.toalsonmarketing.com

To Papaw
We count it all joy

Contents

Life: an Examination
| 3 |

Family: a Meditation
| 83 |

Beauty: a Digression
| 247 |

Identity: a Revelation
| 275 |

Introduction

The book you hold in your hands contains my whole heart. It took me a very long time to gather enough courage to release this collection; in the essay titled "On Childhood Depression," I write about my eight-year-old—he is now eleven. It is a very dangerous, frightening thing to bare yourself as I have done in these pages.

Because several years have passed between the original writings and the publishing of this book, I have a new perspective on many of the essays. For example, the essay titled, "On Surviving the Lean Seasons" ends happily, though I did not know and could not see, at the time of the writing, that it would have a happy ending, which was neither quick nor easy (but no less miraculous). In fact, it took more than two years to see the ending to that essay. (If you'd like to know how it ends, feel free to get in touch; or perhaps I'll write about it again someday.)

I find it valuable to reflect often on where I have been, which always shapes where I am going.

In the pages that follow, you will read about love, family, parenting, depression, tragedy, beauty, faith, and lack of faith, among many other things. I wrote these essays over the course of one year. They are not arranged chronologically but by theme and subject for the purposes of logic and flow.

These essays are stripped-down, naked offerings—windows into my life. I have uncovered my heart, my soul, my honest feelings and philosophies. It is not an easy thing to do, but this is who I am; I am not a perfectly put-together specimen of the female creation. I don't think the world is served by perfection so much as honesty. So I have been honest. For myself. For my family. For you.

At the end of the world, where I have found myself at many points in this journey, I hope we can all say: We count it all joy.

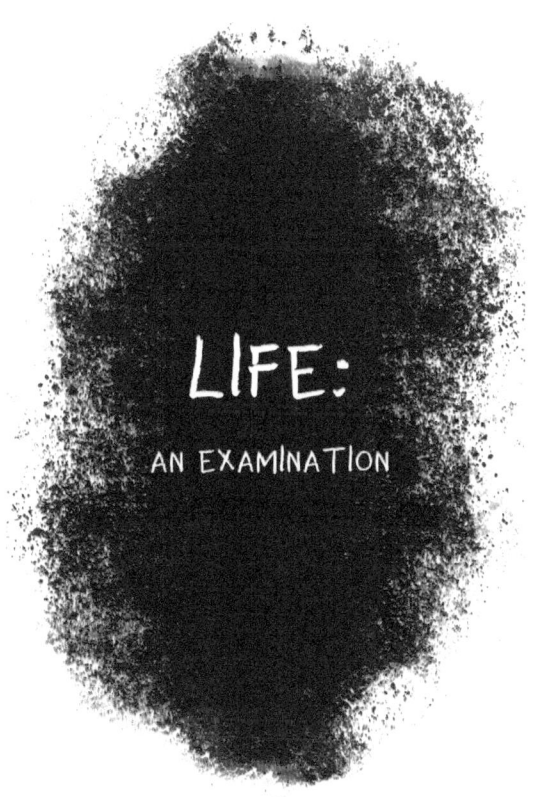

On Anxiety and Depression vs. Faith

It's just a tiny thing, oval and white and smaller than the vitamins I swallow every single day, but I leave it on my desk and stare at it.

It's not the enemy. The panic-lump in my throat is the enemy, and this pill could help. I know this. But still I can't bring myself to touch it.

More than a week ago, my doctor called in a prescription for some of the symptoms I rattled off with an apologetic laugh—lump in my throat, difficulty breathing through some of my thoughts, constant worry—and assured me I was not alone, not even close, because so many people have to take these medications at one time or another.

Yes, but this is me, I thought.

This is me, and I don't take medication to make myself feel better, because I have faith and prayer and meditation and mindfulness and hope and joy and gratitude and love and family and Jesus.

So I let it sit on the pharmacy pick-up shelf long enough for them to restock it, like it didn't belong to anybody in particular, and then I finally drove to the pharmacy to pick it up and a man said he could have it ready in another twenty-four hours because he'd need to fill the prescription all over again. I waited another three days and then sent my husband to pick it up, because I could not face the eyes that would see, notice, judge this woman who needed a pill to feel normal.

Two days it sat on the dresser in my bedroom, waiting, and then, today, when that lump made it hard to breathe, I took one pill out and turned it over in my hands and then let it clink back down to the bottom of an orange bottle.

I can't do it. I can't swallow this pill, because I can find my way out of this. I can. There is nothing wrong with me.

And if there were, what would they all think?

///

When I was eight years old, my teacher noticed I was squinting to read the words on the overhead projector, and then I was squinting at my neighbor's page to copy her notes instead of bothering with the screen at all, and then I was holding multiplication flashcards and books and worksheets too close to my face for comfort. So she told my mom, who talked to the school nurse, who arranged an appointment to check my eyes.

It was a tumultuous time in my life then, because I hadn't seen my father for a year, and those absences explained by an out-of-state job that paid more money than he could possibly make in our little town stretched longer and longer every time he came home and left again. And somehow, in my little-girl mind, my father's absences had become tangled around my perfection or imperfection. Somehow it all depended on me.

Somehow I had to be perfect, and that would bring him home and keep him there for good.

But now something was wrong with my eyes. I knew it before they told me, and I didn't want anyone else to know. I especially didn't want my father to know.

I cried all the way to the nurse's office, because I knew what this appointment would show. I cried standing in front of an illuminated screen, with a little plastic spatula over my left eye, not even able to read clearly the one big lone letter at the top. I cried all the way back out, because my eyes had failed me.

I would never be perfect, and, to an 8-year-old, that meant my father would never come home.

///

I looked for all the reasons not to take that pill. I called my doctor to ask if it was really safe, because I'm a person drawn almost obsessively to natural remedies, avoidant of all toxins, and I've never had this problem before and I don't like medication and there has to be another way, and why isn't this anxiety going away on its own when I'm praying and meditating and working out my salvation and doing everything I'm supposed to do?

What is the source of your anxiety? she said.

So much sits like five-ton weights on my neck and chest and head and feet that drag slow steps through the halls of my home and hands that hold too tightly to control whatever I can control.

I name all the things that flash at random. Work. Kids. Home. Chores. Life.

That's as far as I get, even though I could name money and bills and single-car family and my appearance and my sons, particularly the one struggling with his own depression, and sleep and marriage, too. She interrupts my list and says, *Sometimes we just need help.*

Right before we hang up, she says, *Take care of yourself.*

OK, I say, even though what I really mean is, *I'll try,* because I don't know if taking care of myself is popping a pill or letting it sit with the other fifty-nine of them in a bottle that tells me to swallow one twice a day.

It's another mark of imperfection, this failure of my mind and emotions.

And I don't want anyone to know.

///

My junior high school was eleven miles from the house I grew up in, so I had to ride a bus for an hour every day to get there and back.

In seventh grade I played volleyball and basketball and ran track and sat first-chair clarinet, and every afternoon one or all of these activities had practices I attended, and at the end of those practices, all of us who lived too far away to walk a highway home packed up into a bus and rode it to a drop-off spot where parents waited for pick-up.

We Count it All Joy

There was an evening when I stepped off the bus at 6:30 p.m., just like I did every other weeknight, and I did not see my mom's gray Ford Escort.

The drop-off point was an old post office, where, years before, when we'd lived in another house just down the way, we'd been walking our dog to check the mail and a car going too fast hit our dog (named Chance for his good luck thus far) so hard he spun circles in the middle of the road running between our house and the post office that closed every afternoon at 4.

This particular evening, I sat staring at that same highway, thinking of all the things that could have happened to my mom. Seeing my spinning dog in the middle of the highway, replaced by her tail-spinning car.

I tried to shake off the fears, but what if she'd had an accident coming here to pick me up? What if she was dead? What if it was my fault? Who would the three of us, my brother and sister and me, live with, since we hadn't heard from or seen our dad in a year?

I finally decided I'd walk the eight miles home when my mom pulled into the drive, fifteen-minutes-that-felt-like-fifteen-hours late. The gravel spun under the tires as she came to a stop, and I coughed on the dust, or maybe the emotion, and got in.

I stared out the car window all the way home, trying not to cry as my leftover fears tripped down the highway behind us.

///

I stare out another car window now, trying not to cry, because I don't want my husband or my sons to see just how fragile I feel.

We're on our way to lead worship to a group of teenagers, and I feel like a fraud. We will sing about not being afraid and walking on deep waters with faith ready to be stretched, and here I am sinking in the rip tide of anxiety and fear.

I try to work out some of my feelings with my husband on the way. He tells me I should attempt to put our problems in perspective by considering others' problems. *At least we're not homeless*, he says. *At least we have healthy food in our refrigerator. At least none of our children are terminally ill.*

The rock of anxiety shifts and grows and hardens. *No*, I say. That's not how anxiety works. I feel more anxious now, because what if? What if those things happened? "What if" is the tripwire of an anxious mind. The future is the playground of an anxious mind. Imagining the endless possibilities of what can and might happen are the hazardous snares of an anxious mind. *Stop making it worse*, I want to say, but of course I don't.

He tries another tactic. *Try spinning things in a positive light*, he says, *try nipping your negative thoughts in the bud, try practicing positivity*, but, no, this is also futile for an anxious mind. Every try and subsequent fail simply makes me feel like more of a failure, because I can't do it on my own, and

God why can't I? Why can't I just be happy? Why can't I let it go? Why do these worries and fears circle round and round in an unstoppable dance of fury and fate?

I have a good life. I have a husband who loves me, kids who mean the world to me, a career I would never, ever trade for another.

Why can't I just be happy?

What is it, then? my husband says. *What specifically is it?*

This is the question I can't answer, so I start crying instead. *I can't talk about this right now,* I say, because we've pulled into the parking lot and it's time to unload the kids and go plug in our instruments and do a sound check and then sing like the words and melodies wipe away all our troubles.

And because it's everything.

It's everything, all piled and tangled and curled into those weights with barbs and spikes that puncture me every time something else goes wrong or could go wrong or might possibly go wrong in the next twenty or fifty years.

And sure, I can tick off those gratitude lists and I can try to take every thought captive and I can post those one-hundred-happy-days pictures, but what happens when none of it works, when seemingly simple practices can't and don't save a mind or a heart?

Sometimes we have walked so far down the dark and winding road of not-fine, not-okay, not in a good place, that we need help crawling back to equilibrium.

///

I grew up in two Southern Baptist churches. They were full of grace and hope and people who knew how to love a fatherless kid, or three of them. Southern Baptist, though, is a religion full of rules.

I'd set rules all my life for myself, a personality quirk that served me mostly well, and here, in the middle of religion, were more rules that held a greater purpose. So yes, of course, please sign me up, because keeping all these rules would finally, finally, finally make me perfect in one domain, even though my eyes were bad and I'd busted up my knee in high school volleyball and I'd broken a pinkie finger in softball that never healed straight.

I could be spiritually perfect. That would have to do.

I constructed my perfect little life, keeping all those potential friends in my youth group at arms' length, because if they came too close they would see all the hidden holes in my perfection, and I could not let them see. And then I graduated at the top of my class and rode a full scholarship to university, where, even though all those religion rules had begun weighing me down years ago, I signed up to continue in the Southern Baptist tradition on my own, away from the influence of my mom.

I led worship at the Baptist Student Ministry and attended the Baptist church they told me to attend so I could be a leader, and I sat under all those male preachers who said God was always enough and we had a Healer for all our sickness and that when we know Love we will not know fear.

And I tried to make it true for me.

No one ever told me in those churches that there might be a chance my Healer wouldn't heal the kind of sickness that stuck in the back of a throat and the corner of a mind and froze around the edges of a heart. They only told me to have faith enough to move mountains.

The problem was: this mountain wouldn't move.

///

We are back home and the kids are in bed, and once again I'm sitting here staring at a pill they said I shouldn't need if I believed enough; staring at a piece of science they said proves my faith needs drastic, fundamental improvement; staring at a tiny little thing they said tells a definitive story of my spirituality.

I have learned much in the years that roll between then and now. I have learned that there is a fear that can be known in Love, and it is called anxiety. I have learned that there is a place where joy doesn't come in the morning, and it is called depression. I have learned that taking every thought captive or praying unceasingly or believing that a mountain can move sometimes isn't enough.

I have learned that we don't get to choose our disorders, and no amount of faith or joy lists or gratitude tries can change the hold our disorders keep on us. I have learned that seeking help of any kind for the disorders that rob our lives of joy and hope and peace does not mean our faith or our God or our own hearts and minds have failed us. I have learned that we will not overcome by hiding in a dark room and pretending depression, anxiety, bipolar disorder, schizophrenia, suicide, do not exist for the religiously minded.

I have learned that courage doesn't always look like jumping out of a war-plane into enemy territory or rushing into a burning house or opening a heart to fix a vessel block. Sometimes it looks like staring at the precipice of The End and then facing one more day and then another and then another after that, because this is jumping from a war-plane into enemy territory. Sometimes it looks like braving the truth of our disorder and all the opinions and condemnation and misunderstandings that come with it, because this is rushing into a burning house and living to tell about it. Sometimes it looks like popping a pill and letting it work its magic in our mind, because this is our open-heart surgery.

I have learned that there is no shame in inviting medication into our journey toward healing. The world can make us feel like there is, but the world is not telling the truth. There is no shame here. There is only courage. The Healer sends healing, and sometimes it looks like a miraculous mind makeover, but sometimes it looks like a no-less-miraculous tiny white oval.

So I swallow the pill, and I close my eyes, and I thank

God for the help in finding my way back to an even road, maybe for the first time in my life.

On Hunger

I retype my pastor's words for a story I'm working on, a story I don't even want to finish in these days after learning my job, these eight years of security, will be gone, will vanish in a poof of "downsizing," in less than three months.

Most of us don't know what it's like to be hungry, he said.

And maybe it's true for most. But not for me. I know what it's like to be hungry.

And that's why today, when I mark the ending that stands six weeks before my sixth baby is due, those memories sit like jagged glass shards in the back of my throat, like a fist clamping around my heart, like a sharp iron anchor bending my back and pressing me down, down, down.

I know what it's like to be hungry, and I don't ever want to know again.

///

When I was a girl, eleven years old, I shook out breaded fish sticks and frozen fries from their slightly damp packages and slid them in the oven so my mom didn't have to do it when she got home from the evening job she worked most weekdays after finishing her day as a school librarian. We had the same sort of meal every night, something easy, something we kids could make for ourselves, something carefully divided into the days (thirty of them for the school job, fewer for the night job) that stretched between each paycheck. My mother painstakingly balanced our bills and bought what she could: chicken nuggets, fries, macaroni and cheese, cans of green beans, Vienna sausages, Frosted Flakes, boxes and boxes of Hamburger Helper, and whatever fruit was on sale. I coveted the oranges when we had them; sometimes it was the only thing I'd have for breakfast.

In high school, when my brother would venture out on deep-sea fishing trips, we would blissfully stuff our faces with sautéed tuna or fried flounder or wild shark. But those were more prosperous days, if they could yet be called prosperous, because a stepfather came onto the scene and a one-income household became a two-income one, stabilizing in a way we hadn't experienced for years.

But this was still pre-stepfather time, and my brother and sister and I split the food as well as we could, intuiting, as perhaps all children in those circumstances intuit, that we could not ask for more, even if our bellies were not quite full. More cost more money, and we didn't have more money to spare. There were gas tanks to fill and electricity bills to pay and a phone we needed kept on in case our father happened to call.

There was no food pantry or 4 Million Meals charity

event or income assistantance program for us at that time (though there had been in the past and we still qualified and were permitted free or reduced lunches at school), because pride or bravery or more likely a little of both dictated that my mother do it on her own, without help.

Most nights I climbed into bed with my stomach rumbling in small or large ways, depending on the day and how much month was left between paychecks. I learned to both hide and ignore my hunger.

///

My mother hated being in that hunger place. She hated dividing up a paycheck that was too small and trying to reconcile it with bills that were too large. She would have hated knowing I felt the gnaw of hunger most nights. I thought, at the time, that I mostly succeeded in hiding my hunger, though now that I'm a mother, I'm not sure I did.

This is not what I want for my own children. This is not what I want for myself.

So panic follows me in and out of the rooms of this house my husband and I bought years ago, when jobs were steady and we hadn't yet felt the fear of uncertainty. I walk through the room two boys share and the one twins share and the one my firstborn son claimed as his sleeping-room because it's a library and he loves falling asleep surrounded by books. They are sleeping, no fear or worry or hunger anywhere near those soft, other-worldly faces.

But they are too near mine.

What will we do if we can't take care of them? What will we do if we lose this house that keeps them safe and warm and dry? What will we do if there is not enough food?

These are questions I cannot answer today. These may be questions I cannot answer, either, tomorrow.

///

I stopped eating breakfast and lunch when I was twelve years old. This decision was not a flippant one but an intricately considered one. I tried many times to stop eating, but in the test of will, hunger always won. And then, one day, it didn't.

The reasons for this decision, which seemed rational to a twelve-year-old mind, were, in order of importance: to become and remain thin, to gain some control over something in my life, to avoid moving through the school cafeteria line and risking everyone knowing my family was on the reduced lunch program, and to save my mom the worry of watching the food in our refrigerator disappear faster than she could replace it. All I had to do was curb the hunger, stop eating, and I could save her a little money.

These reasons tangled one around another, until the day I realized I could actually will myself *not* to eat and so began concocting my elaborate excuses that would combat any suspicions of those who might observe my behavior—it was too early in the morning to eat before school or I didn't have time to eat before I rushed out the door—

legitimate, because I was practically always running late to the bus stop. Lunch was somewhat less complicated, since pre-teens tend to be more caught up in their own worlds than others, but I provided my unasked-for excuse anyway: Athletics class was right after lunch, and if we had to run the 1.8 again I was sure to hurl it all up anyway.

But there was another reason I could never say.

What sat at the bottom of that decision, the last factor in a list, was saving my mom the anxiety of opening a refrigerator and seeing it empty again, no oranges, no carrots, no fish sticks or French fries or leftover Hamburger Helper tucked away in its drawers or on its shelves.

Lunch came and went at school, and day after day after day I walked into the school cafeteria with my stomach screaming and then I walked right out to that old oak tree where my friends and I would hang out after they were done eating and I was done pretending. I never stayed in the torture room, my name for the cafeteria, as long as it took my friends to eat, because I couldn't stand to smell all the food I was missing out on.

Someday I would never have to worry about food. That's what I told myself day after day after day. Someday.

///

Except it wasn't so simple, that never having to worry about food.

Maybe we took it for granted all these years we had

steady jobs and extra income and the refrigerator stayed full of good and healthy food, but now, in these days after getting that pink slip about a job ending with the year's ending, in these days of counting seventy-seven days of a job remaining and one hundred twenty-two days until we meet our sixth child, in these days when hunger memories haunt, I feel the panic every time I open the refrigerator.

It turns a world sideways and leaves a mama breathless, and then all those boys come bounding into the room again, looking for something else to eat. And there is food enough today, but what about tomorrow? What about in seventy-seven days, when that job walks away? What about six weeks after that?

My husband follows me around the house, watching me from the corners, trying to convince himself I'm okay, and then, seven days after learning about an ending I don't really want to consider, he throws out his theory about this anxiety I feel and how we attack it by following it to its source.

So what is the source of your anxiety? he says.

I know, but I can't say, not yet, not out loud. I can't say it's losing a home. I can't say it's losing food and health and security. I can't say it's losing kids who need shelter and food and clothes, right along with a parent's love.

I can't say that at the heart of it all is this: I have no more control over our futures.

I can't say all of this yet.

///

It was early on a Christmas morning. It was a sparse year for presents under the tree that year, even though my mother had worked extra shifts for a little Christmas cash. She wanted to do more, but what can a mom do without money?

We were too old to believe in Santa by then. But we heard the bells, and we heard the boots, and we ran to the door to see who might have landed on our old rotted porch with the holes punched all through it.

No one was there. But a box was.

Inside that box were a ham and a turkey and cans of cranberry sauce and green beans and potatoes and already-made pies. That's what I remember, anyway, but maybe the memory has broadened, become more generous in the years since. It seemed to me, at the time, that someone had left a feast on our front porch and then left faster than we could make it to the door. My mom didn't have to look into the eyes of charity, and she couldn't return what she'd been given.

We had more food on our table that day than we had seen in a long, long time, and I allowed myself the simple, guiltless pleasure of eating until I could not eat any more. For the first time in years I went to bed with a stomach that did not toss and turn and rumble.

That meal lasted us days and days and days, and even today, even after all these grown-up years, I still wish I could thank the kind soul who bandaged a mom's heart for Christmas.

///

So what can I do? Fourteen days after tearing that pink slip to pieces in a fit of despair, it is still a question I'm trying to answer, and I can't.

There is a reason for this.

I can try and try and try to figure this all out, and I can try and try and try to secure some kind of hope and future for my family on my own, and I can try and try and try to take control and make a plan and search all those job sites and apply for every one of them, but the truth is that my future is not entirely up to me.

Keeping a house, filling a refrigerator, building a career is not up to me, not really. It's up to a God who planned my every day before I was even born.

That doesn't mean I won't do my part, of course, but it does mean that when the whole world feels like it's turning upside down, when I lose my footing because of an envelope and an unexpected letter, when it feels like I can't find my feet and maybe won't ever again, even then I can rest on One who is more capable than I am.

Security is not an easy thing to surrender, at least not for me. I want to do something. I want to figure it out. I want to try to make it all okay.

But if this experience, this losing a job I thought was secure, has taught me anything at all, it's that the whole world is shaking, and I need a rescue, and I myself am no competent rescuer.

But my God is a rock of peace, and that means I can and will stand again. And again. And again.

It means that even if my kids are hungry, even if we lose the only house we've ever lived in together, even if we're out on the streets sleeping on the blankets I made for each boy's second birthday, we are held. Safe. Still loved. Maybe it's harder to see it from here, in this dark of groping for a handhold or just a foothold that will show me where the next step might be hiding, but I know it to be true, still.

So we go. We follow him into the dark. We brave the weight of all that anxiety, knowing that once our eyes adjust we will see the way forward and through and out again, however messy, uncouth, undignified it looks.

We will still stand, there at the end of the world.

On the Seasons of Life

It's always that time right before dinner is ready, when kids are whining because they're hungry and I'm trying to pour five glasses of milk and no one will set the table like I asked and the soup is boiling over, probably scorching at its bottom because I have no more hands to stir: that time when I'd rather hide in the bathroom and pretend I have disappeared forever than face the disaster of my day.

It's always that window between Family Time and baths, when craft supplies need cleaning up and boys need to be herded upstairs and no one wants to stop in the middle of creating, including their daddy, but I can feel the clock and its best friend, panic, breathing down my neck, because I'm pregnant and don't get to enjoy a glass of wine with dinner currently: that window in which I want to climb under my covers and pretend the whole world, my world, no longer exists.

It's always that string of minutes between an alarm clock chiming and throwing back warm covers: that string of minutes during which I wish, so fervently, that they could get ready for school on their own, without my constant supervision.

And someday they will. But not today.

Today I will pull myself from bed and put their chalkboard schedules beside their bathroom door and I will climb down the stairs in darkness to start the oatmeal, and then I will dish warm goodness into bowls and set them in place and climb back up the stairs to take twins to the potty before everyone comes trampling down to breakfast and the madness really begins.

Today I will dress the littlest ones and help the middle one find shoes that are right in front of his face, and then I will remind the second-oldest to pack up his red folder, and I will climb the stairs once more to pull the oldest away from the LEGO pieces cluttering his room and the books he got at his eighth birthday party last weekend, periodically reminding him that he has only fifteen minutes, ten minutes, five minutes left to eat his oatmeal before it's time to leave.

Today I will walk exhausted and sucked dry and a little overwhelmed because some can't pour milk and some can't tie shoes and some can't put socks on without snagging a toe.

But it will not always be so.

These days of raising five (going on six) boys eight years old and younger, they're not easy, ever, but I have learned something in these years between my own childhood and adulthood. All of life is full of seasons, temporary collections of time on which we will look back, trace the histories of our lives, and wonder at how we made it in one piece or marvel that we were chosen to live it or celebrate how extraordinarily we were changed.

No season will last forever.

///

Just after my first son was born, I had one week of vacation and worked five more weeks from home so I could feed him when he needed feeding and hold him when he needed holding and love him a whole day long. The days were shorter then, and my husband returned home from work just after dark, hopefully in time for dinner.

My baby boy would sleep peacefully in a swing while I watched him from a couch, waiting for his daddy to get home, and the shadows would come crawling in from windows and I would let them, and there was nothing on the table for dinner and nothing I could do about it and nothing I could think about but how we would never get back to the life we had before him. The life of a happily married couple, without children.

Those days before a new baby were filled with spontaneous dates and trips to the grocery store when we wanted spinach dip with French bread and nights of full and sweet sleep. I wasn't ready for this forever change, not even after the eight months I'd had to wrap my mind around it.

And so, on the fourth night after birthing a baby, when my husband came home to a dark living room and a sleeping baby, and when he put his arms around me to feel how my day had gone, I cried into his collared shirt and said the words that had been following me around all day.

Can we give him back? I said. *I'm just not ready.*

He was the perfect baby who slept and smiled and loved his mama hard. But it was new and serious and terrifying, and that old life had passed away while I wasn't looking. I did not expect the new life to be so…hard.

It didn't feel anything like a temporary season in the middle of those dark nights, when a baby cried and a mama cried and a whole world felt like it was crying itself to sleep.

///

Maybe we're not ever ready for the season changes in our lives—because there are new babies and there are lost jobs and there is divorce and sickness and death and pain and grieving, and we want to give it all back. We don't want this season, because, from where we sit, looking out at all the brand new and the unanswered questions and the fear that follows us in and out of days, it feels like this season of waiting, sorrow, disappointment, difficulty might last forever.

Forever is asking too much.

We can't do forever. We can't do every day for the rest of our lives when we can barely even do today, this moment, right now.

It's not easy to step away from those hard days and

remember they will have an end. It's not easy to look at the future without a spouse or a job or our health or the phone calls from our mom or the presence of our dad and see who we are becoming in the middle of the mess. It's not easy to feel sickness or a doctor's question mark or the loss of a baby and know that there is another side to suffering.

But there is. We just have to keep walking or limping or crawling toward that next season.

And if all we can do is lie on the ground and stare at a sky that has turned black and starless, there is hope for us here, too.

A new season will always come to meet us.

///

Almost two months ago my boy, the oldest, was written up at school sixteen times in twenty days for choosing to act outside of who he is, and we had no idea until we were sitting in a principal's office where she shared his conduct violations in quick succession.

There were no signs at home, because he was his same old self, spirited and strong-willed but loving and kind. It was unexpected and heartbreaking, knowing he was becoming the kid other parents warn their kids about.

I cried on the walk home from that meeting, and I burned from the inside out, because hadn't we taught him better, and didn't we have family values, and didn't he know that we loved him more than anything he could ever do?

So why was this happening?

Sometimes there are seasons we would rather not trip through, seasons where a boy is acting out and a school psychologist is called in and an outside therapist is secured, because maybe he'll open up to someone besides a mama and daddy. Sometimes there are seasons where we have to brave the judgment looks of all those other parents, whose kids have probably told them stories about our boy, and we have to remember that our boy is good and kind and wonderfully delightful beneath all the layers of exaggerated stories and misinterpreted intentions and misguided beliefs. Sometimes there are seasons when we will have to look straight in the eye of a teacher who requested a classroom change because she couldn't handle our boy anymore, and we have to know, way deep down, that she doesn't know him like we do.

These seasons can chew us up and spit us out and then leave us to die.

They demand hard work, like digging to the very heart of a hurting little boy who has only ever known brother plus brother plus brother and no identity to call his own. They demand seeing past the surface of behavior into the underground thoughts and beliefs and insights of a child who can feel the stress and anxiety and contempt of others. They ask us to step off a ledge into a darkness we cannot navigate on our own, because the next step is nowhere to be found.

All we want is to get out of seasons like this one,

because they're relentless, and we're afraid, and we really, at the heart of it, simply don't want to fail. Or hurt. Or be destroyed.

Sometimes we need to sit and stay a while.

///

The seasons of life are made to stretch us and squeeze us and recreate us.

There are the exhausting, overwhelming years with children, when we learn how to love in all the hard places. There are seasons when a job is doing well and money is swimming in and everything we touch turns to gold, when we learn humility and generosity, and there are seasons when the gold turns to dust and the job dries up, when we learn faith and hope and even greater generosity in the lean places.

There are the early romance years, when a relationship glides smoothly through rose-colored days and we dream of forever. There are the seasons when love feels like work and it's all we can do to stick around and keep that forever-promise.

There are seasons of friends, when we have support groups propped beneath us and we learn what it means to ask for help and rely on others. There are seasons when friends leave and we must learn to stand on our own.

All of these seasons have something to teach us about life and love and strength and endurance and triumph and truth and courage and wonder.

We won't learn what they have to share if all we ever do is wish this, too, would pass.

///

In thirty days my job will disappear.

We got the pink slip six weeks ago, and I haven't yet done anything about it, because it was unexpected and disappointing and scary. It still is.

On good nights, my husband and I will talk about our creative pursuits and our dreams and everything we're good at, and the whole worlds feels like a huge arena of possibility, and we'll look into the future with excitement and anticipation and hope for the chance to chase dreams. On bad nights I'll crumple into his arms, soggy with tears, because there's the house and all the mouths to feed and a new baby on the way, and what are we going to do? How are we going to make it? What if?

On these bad nights my husband reminds me that we have been here before, in another season of life, when the new felt alarming and the unknown peered in from the dark and the whole world felt like it was coming to an end. We always came out on the other side better versions of our truest selves. We will again.

These seasons, they all come and go. They all rise and fall. They all freeze and then thaw.

And it's only a matter of time before we thaw out of this one, too.

///

We Count it All Joy

So we wait.

Whatever season life sees fit for us, we walk or run or crawl, knowing that we will see our way out of those hardest seasons, but it will take time.

Sometimes there's a summer, where we can hardly find a comfortable place to sit because we're sweating and burning and trying to form a coherent thought in a head that's on fire. But summer gives way to fall, when the air lightens and we can send kids outside and the whole world feels kind and hopeful and full of harvest and thanks and warm goodness. And then it all turns white and cold and we can only shiver in bed or shiver to breakfast or shiver through a whole didn't-go-like-I-expected-or-wanted day because branches are cracking and breath is frosting and death of all that is beautiful is coming with a vengeance.

But life waits underneath it all, and it bursts forth in a new day, when we can breathe full and deep again, and what was frozen is purposed anew, wearing green.

We are recreated in all these seasons. And none of them last forever.

Those anxiety pills you're on? You won't take them forever. Those problems you're having with your boy? You won't have them forever. Those mornings you feel sucked dry by all the child-leeches in your house? They won't last forever. The disagreement you had with your mother-in-law? It won't last forever. The depression that knocks you to your knees? It won't last forever. The sickness tying you

up in knots? It won't last forever.
    Life, after all, can change in a moment.

On New Years

Five days I had been sick, and nothing would come out right, and I felt tired and cranky and frustrated that even after all this time my eyes still burned and my throat still felt like it was holding shards of glass and my nose was the heaviest appendage on my face, except for my ears when I tried to lie down and sleep.

All the hours before this particular one in which I was lying, unable to move, on my bed, I had been trying to rally myself, suck it up, do *something*, because it was the last week of winter break for the two boys in school, and I didn't get to spend much quality time with them when school was in session. But all I really wanted to do was stay in bed, alone, and rest until I could hold up my head without the whole world spinning.

They'd been watching movie after movie, because it was too cold and wet outside. The whole house was falling apart, since I couldn't bring myself to care. And for that, and much more, guilt shadowed my heels, whispering a variety of things, but the loudest was this: I was not being a mama to my boys, I was just lounging on a couch hoping the movie would keep them fully entertained until lunchtime and I could summon the effort to climb from those piles of blankets and fix them something healthy that I wouldn't want to eat because I hadn't been able to taste anything since Sunday.

It was not how I wanted to ring in a new year.

///

Weeks ago we'd made our plans to sit out in our cul-de-sac to watch the neighbors set off their fireworks, and we'd intended to catch up on their holiday news and their hopes for the new year, like we always do. We were going to let boys stay up later than usual, because fireworks are exciting and beautiful, and the noise of them would keep them all up, so why not? And before all that, we were going to sit and talk about some goals for the new year, as a family, and then we were going to solidify some other goals, as a couple. But I can't seem to stop sniffling and sneezing and hacking up whatever is hanging out in my chest.

I guess I, perhaps a little too optimistically, hadn't expected to start a new year with a filthy house and an early date with the bed and a miserable cold or flu virus that would probably, in the next few days, work its way right along to the other three in my family who haven't had it yet. (Sickness doesn't readily lend itself to optimism.)

It's disappointing to end an old year with sickness and ring in a new one with that same unwelcome sickness.

We have all these expectations for what the days or weeks or the whole new year is going to look like, and then there are all these setbacks and unknown variables that come sweeping in, even in the first few hours, and it's hard to know what to do with them when we are clinging so tightly, with iron fists, sometimes, to the way we *wanted* things to be.

It wasn't so much the sickness that felt disappointing in that first day of a new year. It was, more accurately and somewhat more simply, the shattered expectations.

///

Somewhere along my life journey, I began to connect the way we rang in a new year with the way a whole new year would go. It sounds silly, but it's actually astonishing how these subtle little inaccuracies can creep into an otherwise rational mind. If we rang in a new year jobless, I couldn't help but worry that's how the whole next year would go. If we rang it in tired or frustrated or disappointed in the way the last year had gone, that's how the whole next year would go, too. If we rang it in sick, we could expect sickness in the next year.

I was a regular self-proclaimed prophet, at least in my unconscious mind.

Over the years, I have let that belief exert a whole lot of pressure on me, so I always tried to start a new year with a perfectly clean and tidy house (because who wants to spend the whole next year in a dirty, out-of-control one?). I always tried to patch up relationships with bosses (because who wants bad communication at the job for the whole next year?). I tried to shake off my anxiety, for at least the one day that turned into a new year (because who wants anxiety hanging around for a whole new year? I would learn, eventually, that anxiety was here to stay, a disorder in my brain).

This particular year beat them all, because there was a job ending and anger aimed at the people who had chosen to end it two weeks before a new baby will be born, and there was anxiety about the future and a big black hole of unknown sitting on top of all those new months of a year, a calendar of wide open nothing (I could have seen it as possibility, but I am nothing if not stubbornly consistent in my thought patterns during depressive days: my world is usually on its way down).

And then sickness on top of it all.

What kind of year would the next year be, with all of these dark spots already showing up? What chance did it have, in the shadow of all this?

These questions walked me right into the new year, though I was sleeping, worn out from worry and nose-blowing in about the same capacity, when they did.

///

There was another year when sickness rang in a new year.

It was a plague, several years ago, a stomach virus that wouldn't leave us be. Forty days we fought it, forty days of scrubbing toilets and washing blankets and soaping up hands until they were chapped and raw, and then came the day when no one puked or dirtied their pants, and I started finally, tentatively, hoping that, for God's sake, it was over.

We were creeping up on a new year, and I wanted to be virus-free when that clock said 2010 had turned into 2011.

Two days down, and I thought for sure we were in the clear. Three days with no vomit or diarrhea and I braved going to church for the first time in more than a month, and then as soon as we walked in, my twenty-month-old, holding to the side of his five-month-old brother's stroller, bent over and heaved all over the gymnasium floor.

Well. I would be marking a new year with a washer full of blankets and soiled clothes, just like I'd spent the last forty days.

I cried in those shocked moments, partly because I was mortified but mostly because I couldn't do it anymore; I had reached the end of my rope and there was no more slack. I took a deep breath, walked them all back out the door, and listened to the oldest, four years old at the time, screaming that he wanted to stay at church with Daddy because we hadn't been able to leave the house in too many days.

I wanted to scream, too. But instead I let him go and took the sick and the potentially sick one home.

It will never be over, I thought. *This plague will ruin the whole of 2011. We will never recover from this beginning-of-the-year setback.*

And we almost didn't.

///

I don't want to be this person anymore. It's a silly way to live. Just because something is plaguing us when the old year turns to new doesn't mean it has the power to define the whole next year. That's a lie that keeps us afraid and timid and ineffective.

One day does not mean a whole year down the drain. Two days don't mean a whole year down the drain. Two hundred days don't mean a whole year down the drain.

Half the picture doesn't tell the whole story.

So much of what we do and accomplish in life, so much of our success or our failure, hangs completely on our attitude about it all. We can meet those setbacks with defeat already on our minds and clenching our hearts, and they will be our defeat. Or we can meet those setbacks with grace, and they can turn into a year of learning all there is to know about resilience and positivity and choosing gratitude in the hardest of places, and they can be our victory.

Sometimes it's easy to forget, in the middle of trying times—when we're laid up in bed too sick to talk and someone forgot to pay the water bill and the checkbook hasn't been balanced in thirty days, maybe more—that it's not about what a year can do to us so much as it is about what we can do to a year.

We are stronger than we know. We are braver than we know. We are more resourceful than we know.

Life is not something that happens to us. It is something we can mold and steer and change, with the proper tools, the backbone of support, and a mind that can turn from wide open nothingness to wide open possibilities.

Even if the way my new year had started, with lingering sickness and question marks surrounding the employment piece and hours of playing games and doing puzzles and watching movies with my older sons while the younger ones slept, is the way the whole year that followed went (and it didn't, of course), what's so bad about that? What's so bad about spending a whole year learning how to rest and trusting our future to God's hands and practicing staying present with the little ones we love, who won't be little forever? What better way to live a year than fully present in the moment, like that New Year's Day demanded of me?

It's a powerful, empowering thought.

On Home

It was so unexpected, the way it showed up.

There was someone staying with us, someone helping out in those crazy days of adjustment, someone who burned the side of a chair because of a not-thinking mistake, and when I came downstairs in the early morning after a night I smelled melting microfiber but was too exhausted to investigate, I ran my hand along the ugly, startling black of an arm that should have been cream, and I cried.

And cried and cried and cried.

It was silly, really, the crying. It's a chair. A possession. Something that means so little in the grand scheme of things. But I cried because it can't be fixed, because it's a whole black arm, because we've tried so hard to keep pieces of our life normal and nice and presentable, and it's next to impossible with six rowdy boys, and this destruction wasn't even done by one of the children but by someone who knows what a hot pot can do to fabric and simply had a moment of amnesia.

It felt like reality giving me a big, fat slap in the face.

You will never have or keep or make anything that will survive destruction, it said. *Don't you remember the choices you've made?*

You will never not be embarrassed to have the neighbors over, it said. *Don't you remember where you come from?*

You will never have a nice home, it said. *Don't you remember who you are?*

In my home there are holes in walls and milk splatters on doors and dining room chairs with loose legs we can't trust will hold us when we sit. There are mirrors with perpetual finger smudges and plants that are dying and carpet that has seen much better days.

There is now a favorite armchair with a blackened arm.

This is a home that is shabby and ragged and worn out. This is a home I would like to change. Make better. Beautify.

///

The first home I remember I see only in flashes, a trailer in a sunny place with a playground, or what in a child's mind qualified as a playground, in the backyard, or somewhere close, where my brother and I would kick our feet high enough to reach the sky. It was bright and small and charming.

And then there was a home across the street from a school, where I watched my brother walk out the door at the beginning of a day and then walk back in at the end, knowing he'd sit and teach me all he'd learned in his kindergarten class.

In this home I remember a playroom where my mom found a snake in our toy box and ran out of the room screaming so we all chased her like it was some kind of game. I remember sharing a room with my brother and sister, a room where I once accidentally rolled from the top bunk where my brother slept and hit the floor so hard I couldn't even cry, could only lie there on hardwood and try to remember how to breathe.

I remember seeing my mom hacking snakes into pieces with a hoe and listening to someone playing piano so it echoed through the wood-floor living room and watching my dad driving away on a motorcycle and the way the yellow curtain above the front door swished, swished, swished, until I could not hear the spatter of his engine anymore, the way it felt like I'd just fallen from the top bunk again, because his leaving hit me so hard I couldn't cry, could only lie there and try to remember how to breathe.

This home was dark and light and sad and funny and ugly and beautiful and full of paradox.

///

There was another home with magnolias in the front yard and so many pecan trees in the back that my Nana would pay us to gather them when she came to visit, and because it was money and it was for Nana's pecan pie, we'd do it for hours and hours, bringing in buckets of pecans. I remember forts in climbing trees and a tire swing we'd use to make our kittens dizzy, watching them walk and laughing until we cried. I remember blackberries we'd soak in milk and sugar for an afternoon snack.

I remember sitting on my dad's lap with a bowl of cucumbers soaked in vinegar, and I remember the dark hallway I could never walk down, only sprint down, and I remember birthday parties with lines of kids playing Red Rover and getting clotheslined by the solid wall of two clasped hands.

This home was chipped and wobbly and not quite secure, in a way that could not be explained, like the old porch swing that hung out front.

///

The years turn a little hazy after that, because there was a move out of state and a move back, and those homes were unexpected and upsetting and lonely.

There was the one in Ohio, where I slipped down cement stairs the day of my birthday and tore my new pantyhose all the way down the leg; where my brother and sister and I came home to an empty house after school and locked all the doors tight behind us, because there was no money to pay someone to watch us and it wasn't exactly the best neighborhood; where I slept every night with a doll I'd had since I was a baby, even though I was too old for dolls, resting the back of my hand on her cool face and pretending I couldn't hear my mom and dad fighting through the walls.

It was the home that told us the truth about a man we loved and another woman and a baby on the way, all laid out on an answering machine because someone thought we should know. It was the home that said life would never be the same. And it wasn't.

That home led to another home, one we shared with a grandmother, because a divorce was coming. I don't remember much of this home, only frustration and resentment and a bitter root that had to be carved out, years later. I remember a brother with ulcers and a mom who had to work too much and three kids once more squished into one room, even though they were all too old to share. I remember pinecones and watching out a window to see who would be home first, Mom or Memaw, and Metallica blasting from an open garage, speaking what we could not.

That home was cold and uneven and hard, like the sidewalk out front where we would roller blade for hours, just to get out of the tension that threatened to break us all.

///

My last childhood home is the one where my parents still live today.

The day we moved in, the windows had a film of dirt so thick you could hardly see through them. The carpet was rust-colored and shabby and smelled ancient. The porch bent in the middle.

I remember feeling afraid to bring my first boyfriend there, because surely he wouldn't want to be with someone as poor as me. I remember, for the first time, not wanting to have my birthday parties at home, because what would all those classmates think? I remember wishing I lived in her house or in his or in that one so much nicer than mine.

I was ashamed of that home.

It didn't matter that this home held memories of a sister falling asleep in the closet while she was dressing for school and how we laughed about it so hard we were crying, for the first time in years. It didn't matter that it held the miracle of a brother walking the road to a canal where he would fish and find himself. It didn't matter that it held the victory of a mother who groped her way back through the dark.

It didn't matter that it held a second chance in all its rickety, peeling walls.

All I could see, then, were those holes in the porch and the way the front door stuck when we tried to open it and all the dirt and dust still left in the corners after hours of trying to scrub it clean.

All I could see was what glared from the outside.

///

All I can see in my home is what glares from the outside, too. Holes in walls. Splatters on doors. A burned arm on a cream chair. Especially that.

But in all these days after, the truth of home begins to bloom.

Home is not a place. It's not four walls and a roof and

perfectly arranged and preserved furniture. It's them, my family. It's me. It's a heart-space.

Home cannot be contained. It is carried. Given. Received.

I can see it all the way through the time line of a life, the leavings, the moves, the starting-overs. Home never changed, even though those houses did, year after year.

Home is love—overwhelming, pure, unbridled, burning the arms of a mama wrapping all her boys in hugs.

Sure, I might grieve the destruction of that favorite chair, because it's real, and it can't be fixed, at least not right now, and it will always stare at me from a room inside my house, but it does not tell the whole truth of my home. It never will. Home is more than a chair where a mama fed all her babies.

Home is an eight-year-old writing a sweet, sweet note to his little brother, and it's a five-year-old helping a twin put on shoes so he can play outside, too, and it's a two-year-old saying that what he's thankful for tonight is his mama's beautiful eyes, even though she spoke a little too harshly to him half an hour ago. Home is a husband making his wife lunch every single day, because he knows she won't take the time to eat unless he does, and it's a four-year-old playing Battleship with a brother, and it's a last baby grinning at a mama in the early morning hours, when no one else is awake.

This home is radiant and wild and free. It is lovelier

than any home we could build with two hands and a bank full of money.

And I am so glad I get to live here.

On Joy

Just a few days ago, I got a precious letter from a reader, thanking me for one of my essays. She found it because she was looking, because she'd just lost two babies, twins, and she needed some comfort.

I have written many versions of this story, about the daughter who died before I could meet her, because writing is my way of working through something hard and unthinkable and tragic. Writing is my way of finding my feet again.

The day they wheeled me into the operating room, where they sucked a dead baby from my uterus in the same way they take live ones from the women who don't want them, I wrote the pain onto my phone until the anesthesia knocked me out. And then I started writing again as soon as I woke, when the agony of an empty womb ran red and bled through my fog.

I wrote in all the days after. All the months after. All the years after.

And now, three years later, there is a woman searching for comfort, and she finds my words, and she feels less alone in her sorrow, even though we are thousands of miles apart.

We Count it All Joy

We count it all joy.

We count it all joy that a day as sorrowful as that one could do this: Heal another heart, or at least some small piece of it.

///

The year I turned eleven a letter came in the mail for my mother. It told her secrets she had known for years but didn't dare believe, because even in the humiliation, even in the shame, even in the disappointment, she still loved.

The letter told a story of a man and a woman and a child and a baby on the way. It told the truth of heartache and betrayal. It told the future of a single mother.

She didn't feel brave enough to become what the letter said she must, but she did. She filed for divorce and bought a house with the last of her savings and got a second job so she could raise her kids on her own.

It wasn't all neat and pretty, because she was lonely and heartsick and sad, and sometimes it was near impossible to see a way out of the mess. But she put one foot in front of the other and marched on, like a heroic woman warrior, because she had three kids who needed food and shelter and both a mother and a father—and she would play the father for a time.

There came a woman, years later, who visited her Sunday school class, who broke into tears when the leader asked for prayer requests, who could barely say what she needed to say about leaving a husband and two kids to feed and not really knowing how or if she would make it on her own.

And my remarkable mother knew the answer to this woman's wondering.

Yes, she said. *Yes, you can make it. And here is how.*

The real miracle of it is that my mother, in comforting another woman who had lived the same story, found her way fully into forgiveness.

We count it all joy.

///

It's not easy, this counting it all joy—because there is a baby who died, and there is a husband who is husband no longer, and how can this dark night turn to sun-bright day?

Maybe it's hard to see from the suffering side of it, that our pain will one day, months or years or decades from now, be used to comfort another ripped-in-two heart. Maybe it doesn't seem fair that we would have to endure death and divorce and abandonment and shame and disappointment and fear and pain and anxiety and heartbreak so that one day down the road we can walk someone else through their own.

Maybe we wouldn't choose it for ourselves, not in a million years.

But all those maybes don't change the truth: that our sorrow places, those chasms cut with knives that plunge deep, are the very places we can be filled with the deepest joy. Of course it's hard, and of course it's unwanted, and of course we would never dream of asking for the opportunity to suffer, but this is life and this is unfair and this is what happens when we choose to risk and love and live.

In the sorrow places we learn how to live with our hearts wide open. Our lives wide open. Our selves wide open.

We learn how to count it all joy.

///

When my third son was born, our pediatrician, an amazing, empathic man, breezed into the room and shook my husband's hand, pulling him into an embrace, because he was, genuinely, so excited that another Toalson boy had slipped into the world. And then, when the congratulations were done, he took out his devices to look over the baby.

The air in the room shifted when he listened to my boy's heart. He tried to act like it wasn't a big deal, but I could see the alarm in his eyes.

"It sounds like there's a murmur," he said, and he looked at my husband, not me, because he knew, *he knew* what those words would do to me. "It's probably just one of the valves that hasn't closed up yet. Sometimes that happens. It'll likely correct itself." He put his devices away and then said, like an afterthought, "Come see me in another week so we can make sure."

It didn't correct itself.

He referred us to a specialist, and it was two weeks of

dreaming about a boy whose lips turned blue while I watched and there was absolutely nothing I could do about it. Two weeks of agony, waiting for that appointment, waiting for someone to tell me if something was wrong with my baby boy's heart.

    I would put my older boys down for their nap, and I would hold my newborn while I should have been sleeping, because sleep was the least important thing in the world if I had to say goodbye. I would pull him into bed with me at night, because I was so afraid it would be the last night. I would cook dinner, holding him in my arms, my tears dropping into the chicken noodle soup.

    And then, finally, finally, finally, came the appointment. I took my infant into the room while my husband stayed with our other two sons in the decked-out waiting room full of toys. This was a heart doctor for children with heart defects. The waiting room was amazingly entertaining.

    I sat beside the doctor and her assistant, who was there to hold down the babies who decided they didn't want to do an echocardiogram. She warned me I might have to help hold him down, but my boy slept right through it.

    He slept through a doctor pointing out all the perfection, running her finger along the lines of arteries that pumped and pulled blood. He slept through a mama sobbing because of the incredible, miraculous beating of a tiny little heart, pulsing on a screen, lighting up with red and blue, the colors of life. He slept through a mama sobbing harder, if possible, when the doctor said, "Perfectly healthy. Nothing to worry about here."

"I'm sorry," I kept saying. "I'm sorry. It's just..."

I couldn't even find the words for something so big and yet so small, but the doctor understood. Of course she did. She sees it all the time, these tiny veins and tiny organs and tiny perfection pieces keeping a baby alive. She patted me on the arm and sent me out the door with the words, "Go enjoy your healthy baby boy."

And I did.

A year later, a friend's daughter was born with what doctors suspected was a murmur. I knew what it was like. I knew the agony of waiting and the torture of anxiety and the way worry can take a whole birthing day and wring the life right out of it.

So I shared my story. I let her know she was not alone in her fear, that someone else had walked her shoes, that she was not forgotten or unseen but known in her suffering.

We count it all joy.

///

There is a catch here, too. Of course there is.

We can suffer in silence. We can crawl into our shells and pretend life is grand and we have not a care in the world, and we can show them that worry and anxiety and suffering do not touch us.

We can grieve secretly, alone, in our closed-off places.

It's more comfortable there, because our shells are thick and dark and hidden, and "they" don't have to know that we questioned the purpose of life when our baby died, and "they" don't have to know that we worried we would not make it as a single mom of three kids, and "they" don't have to know that we doubted the very existence of God in the moments we thought our boy could die.

Or we can set those secrets free. We can let our sorrow loose to light up the world, transform it completely. The beautiful piece of sorrow is that the darker it looks on this side of it, the brighter it turns on the got-through-it side.

How do we let loose our sorrow?

We share. We tell our stories. We carry on.

We're not the first or the last to walk through this specific sorrow space, but it is only in our sharing that we see clearly that we are never alone. That we can bear each other's burdens. That we can heal, together.

That we can count it all joy.

On the Freedom of Speech

All day long I've been checking comments and shaking my head and feeling distracted by this war happening online, on my space, so I didn't get much work done.

Many of the comments are kind, but too many of them are not. So I sit down to my computer and get ready to fire back my responses. Something about how we should take care with our words and assumptions and especially strangers' hearts.

My husband puts his hand on my arm. "It's not worth it," he says. "You can't argue with people like that. You just have to ignore them."

I scan the tirade one more time, and every single one of them pouring poison online holds up a "freedom of speech" card, claiming their right to share their opinion. And yes, it's true. We do have the right to our own opinion. But just because we have the right to free speech and the freedom of expression, does that mean we should use it to air everything we think?

This is a harder question to answer.

///

When I was eleven years old, I stood outside the little Baptist church I attended on Wednesday nights and watched a friend play basketball with some of his older buddies.

Another girl watched, too. She had a crush on my friend, but he didn't ever pay any attention to her, mostly because he had a crush on me. I didn't see him as anything more than a friend, so I kept trying to bring them together. But my efforts didn't work.

And there came a day when the youth leader called us all inside and the boys went one way and the girls went another, and my friend hugged me and said he was leaving early and wouldn't see me again until school the next morning.

The girl was watching. The boys disappeared, and she turned to me and said, "You have a really pointy nose." Then she walked away.

Maybe it wouldn't have affected me as much if my dad hadn't just left my family for another one. Maybe I wouldn't have been as bothered if I hadn't already been uncomfortable in my skin. Maybe I could have let it go if I hadn't already been walking my way toward eating disorders and wishing I were different.

I can't say for sure, because that wasn't my reality then.

I tried to pretend her words hadn't hurt me as much as they did. I tried to keep my fingers from tracing the shape of my nose. I tried to walk past the girls' bathroom without ducking inside.

But I did go inside, and I stood looking at my nose in

the mirror for five whole minutes, turning to examine it from every angle.

Yeah, I thought. *Yeah, I see what she means. It* is *pointy.*

If she thought it was pointy, how many other people did, too?

///

Even today, in my dark days, when I find myself unhappy with my appearance, her voice joins the others in their raucous chorus.

What does it matter? you might say. What does it matter what one little girl thought? What does it matter what other people think? You shouldn't be so weak to care. You shouldn't be so insecure about yourself that the words of another person can hurt you.

The problem is that we are all, at the heart of us, wired for connectivity. What exercising our freedom of speech and our right to our own opinions through personal attacks on other people does is it disconnects us from the human experience of community. It casts outside the circle the ones being attacked.

The Universal Declaration of Human Rights was adopted by the United Nations General Assembly in 1948. It was the first global expression of the basic human rights all people could claim. Freedom of speech was added as Article 19 in 1949. Article 19 said that "Everyone has the right to freedom of opinions without interference and to seek, receive and impart information and ideas through any media and regardless of frontiers."

This idea of free speech and expression had been developing since the advent of the printing press. Traditionally, governments had limited printing opportunities to only those materials that the government agreed with. Because of this limitation, political ideas could not be freely debated.

Free speech and the free expression of ideas was originally a political, intellectual right, not a personal one meant to justify airing our opinion about everything.

Governments still restrict freedom of speech and expression based on the harm principle, which says that one's freedom cannot be used to harm another. Some of those restrictions include libel, slander, hate speech, fighting words, and oppression. There are many others.

Article 19 also states that the freedom of speech and expression carries "special duties and responsibilities…for respect of the rights or reputation of others."

This is the part we seem to have forgotten.

///

In college I worked as the editor-in-chief of the college newspaper. There were a few rotating cartoonists who would publish editorial cartoons with us.

One night a cartoonist turned in his cartoon, and I immediately had a bad feeling about it. In the cartoon, a professor stood at the front of the class. A bubble above him said, "Blah, blah, blah." The students around him all had hostile expressions on their faces. Some were sleeping. A few were throwing things at him. One, I seem to remember, had a gun, though I'm not entirely sure my memory hasn't fabricated this detail, perhaps made the cartoon worse than it really was because of what happened later.

I called the cartoonist to see if he had anything else he could send me.

"Why?" he said.

Because this one didn't seem very respectful, I said.

"It's not a real teacher," he said. "It's just a joke. It's a humorous opinion."

He said he had nothing else to give me, and I was two hours from deadline with nothing else to fill the space.

So I let it run.

The next afternoon, when I got to my office, my voice mailbox was full. My email was inundated. People were outraged by the cartoon. It shouldn't have run.

It seemed that everyone but me knew who the professor was, because even though the name had been changed in the cartoon, the picture, they said, was a dead giveaway.

I had to not only submit a formal apology for letting something so insensitive print in the paper for which I was responsible, but I also had to fire a really good cartoonist who'd probably just been annoyed at a teacher for some reason or another and decided to lash out in the best way he knew how.

Just because we have freedom doesn't mean we should use it.

///

With this freedom comes great responsibility.

We are responsible for our words and whether they build up or tear down. We are responsible for the hearts of one another.

In this day of computer communication, with our ever-increasing ability to comment anonymously all over the Internet, we have gotten really good at firing off responses, without really thinking about how, at the other end of our words, there is a real, breathing person.

We can't see their face. We don't know much about their lives. We assume the parts that are missing.

It's easy to forget our responsibility.

I don't have a problem with a friendly exchange of ideas, with a person who can respectfully disagree with what I have to say, someone who makes a good effort to convince me of his or her viewpoint without feeling the need to make it personal. But when someone starts attacking me or the members of my family, saying destructive, hurtful, dishonoring things they have no way of knowing for sure, that's when they have lost their ability and their right to communicate with me.

What freedom of speech really means is expressing our opinions or viewpoints in a way that does not damage other people or people groups. It means carefully weighing our words and running them through a filter—is it kind? Is it true? Is it necessary?—and only speaking when our words pass the test. It means seeking harmony and peace even in disagreement.

We cannot claim our right if we do not exercise our responsibility.

Freedom of speech has the ability to broaden our minds in astounding ways, introducing us to new ideas and uncomfortable viewpoints and enriching humanity's full experience of life.

We just have to know how to use it.

On Surviving the Lean Seasons

We've just gotten back from the doctor, because, for days, my throat has held barbed wire or shards of broken glass, and my fever is out of control and I've lost two work days to sleep.

We're turning onto the street that leads to our house, shaking our heads at the strep throat diagnosis, when the air conditioner on the van—the only vehicle we have—stops working, and a noise starts following us home.

A noise that means something is wrong with our van.

My husband spends hours trying to figure out how to take out an old, messed-up compressor and put in a new one—a new one he bought with a credit card, because God knows we don't have it in our checking account.

All this after breaking a foot and having sick kids and logging two months without any steady income, just side jobs here and there, and I tell a friend, "Sometimes I feel like the universe is just throwing one thing after another in our path, asking us how resilient we are. And all I want to do is hold up my middle finger."

Five months ago we had our sixth baby. Two days after he slid into our lives, I was laid off my job. We blew through the severance (since the job never paid that much anyway). There used to be savings, because I always obsessively saved, making sure we lived on the lowest dollar possible so we could hide money away for a moment like this one. But here we are, with that buffer nearly gone, and fixing the car will take more than we've pulled in this month. Again.

My anxiety is so high I have a panic attack every time I think about the electric bill and the mortgage and what it takes to feed six boys in the summer. Usually those attacks come late at night, when I'm trying to fall asleep and those ugly words wrap around my neck: *How are we going to do this?*

I feel sad and terrified. Mostly I feel angry. Angry that we're here, angry that the plans we believed were God's plans don't seem to be working, angry that God's promises don't apply to us.

We didn't use our money selfishly. We gave generously to the church. Even now, even when we're pulling in zero income ($300 on a good month), we're supporting some missionary friends and six World Vision kids so they can have a better future—because no matter how quickly it makes the backup money run out, I can't stop doing it. I can't.

We've given everything to follow the call God put on our lives, and yet here we are, talking about the very real possibility of selling our house to keep ahead of the bank. I've never felt so angry in my life.

///

A month ago, I walked up to the front of my church, where those prophetic prayer people waited, and I swallowed the pride that gets in the way of asking for help, and I asked for help. Prayer this time. I could handle asking for prayer, if only barely. More than prayer? No way.

"I get this picture that you are not sitting at God's feet waiting for an answer," said one of the women, a good friend of mine. "I see you grabbing onto his collar and screaming your desperation into his face."

I just nodded, not daring to speak, because, yes, that's exactly what I did that morning. Exactly what I've done every morning for the last four months. Shouted at him. Screamed at him. Cried, raged, begged.

And every morning there is NOTHING.

My friend also said there was such great pain in this foggy season not because the money wasn't steady (or there, really), but because something in my childhood had felt exactly like this, too. And at first I tried to ignore that piece of it, because what's important now is trying to figure out a way to feed my family, not trying to heal some old childhood wound.

We got home, and it was time to balance the checkbook, and I opened the email with the electric bill. The bill was $143.18.

An old friend of ours used to believe the numbers 143 were God's way of communicating with us across time and space. *I love you*, they said. *143*. But there was a bill and a checkbook that didn't have enough money to pay it, and what did that mean for me?

I started crying, shaking my head, saying the only thing I could think to say. "But do you really, God? Because this doesn't feel like love. It feels a whole lot like abandonment."

Sometimes numbers are just numbers.

///

When I was just a girl, three years old, or four, maybe, my mom and dad took my brother and sister and me to a water park. Or maybe it was just a neighborhood pool. My memory gets fuzzy with some of the details. Others are crystal clear.

My sister was a baby, so she stayed off to the side with my mom, while my dad told my brother and me that we could go down the massive slide on the other side of the pool. It was a tunnel slide, with all kinds of twists and turns. I watched my brother slide down so my dad could catch him. I was content to watch, too afraid to try. But my dad wanted me to try.

He walked me to the top, sat me on his lap, and wrapped his arms around me. He said, "I won't let you go." Then we were tearing down the slide, and the bottom was getting too close, and I was screaming terror.

A tower of water slammed into us. And my dad let go. He let go.

///

He would let go in other ways over the years. There would be the day he decided he wanted a new family and all those days after, passing without a single word from him. There would be birthdays and graduations and an aisle I would walk down on the arm of my stepfather, who was as proud as any father could be.

When a parent leaves and doesn't look back, what he's saying is, *Figure it out on your own.*

Figure it out on my own. How I wish I could.

It's not surprising that I would have this picture of God, too. That there were more important people for him to be concerned with. That I did not matter in the lineup of human beings who needed him. That he could not be bothered with remembering my birthday or paying my mortgage or making sure my kids were cared for.

And then came this last son, born the day before my birthday so God could remind me that, look, he gave me the greatest gift a mama could ever get: another son. I was not forgotten.

Except all those months came after his birth, and, with them, hit after hit after hit, and I could barely lift my head from the floor, because this didn't feel like love.

THIS DOESN'T FEEL LIKE LOVE.

I feel abandoned. I feel forgotten. I feel wrong, like maybe we were selfish to have so many children or pursue our dreams or try to build our own businesses or use our gifts or make a way where there was no way.

We Count it All Joy

I certainly don't feel brave, the kind of brave needed for something like this. I feel like a little eleven-year-old girl who's wondering if her daddy is going to come through for her.

And he never did.

///

We did not plan for everything.

Some would say we made our bed and now must figure out how to fit in it. And maybe it's true. We chose to have six children, even though we could not have seen what might happen two days after our sixth was born. We chose to turn down that job offer my husband got a year ago because we thought we needed to stay at our church and heal a little. We chose to believe that God would take care of our needs instead of planning how to afford six kids on paper.

Now I can't help it. I feel cornered and trapped—and that makes me fighting-angry.

On my best days I shape thousands and thousands of words into essays and songs and poems and stories. On my worst days I sit around thinking maybe we shouldn't have had so many children.

Which one would I have given back? That answer's easy at least. Not one of them.

All my life I've heard these stories of other people falling on hard times and then—miracle of all miracles—that giant check comes just in time at the end of the month, and there you go.

There you go. All neat and pretty. They're blessed people. And if they're blessed people, then that makes us… not blessed people—because on the last day of last month, we transferred half the remainder of our savings into our checking account to pay for our most basic needs, make sure our kids had food to eat, keep a roof over our heads for another month.

"It's so hard to understand," I told my mom the next day. "After so many years of giving ourselves to God's mission and ministry."

Makes a person not ever want to do mission and ministry again. That's the part I didn't say out loud.

///

"God will provide," they say. "God will make a way where there is no way," they say. "Don't worry about tomorrow," they say. "God will meet your needs."

What about when he didn't? When he still doesn't?

Does that make him any less sovereign? Any less great? Any less merciful or loving or kind?

My head wants to say yes. Yes, it makes him less sovereign, great, merciful, loving, kind. Yes, it makes him cruel and uncaring and just like the earthly father who let go.

But my heart knows the answer.

No. God is the same today as he was yesterday. He does not change because of my circumstances or my feelings or even my knowledge or lack of it.

So what does all this mean?

Well, I wish I had a neat and pretty answer for you. But I don't, because our story isn't over. We are still navigating through this mess, and we don't know how it's going to end. Not yet.

All I know for sure today is that love sometimes does what's better instead of what's easier. My kids remind me of that every day.

I guess I know something else, too. One day the anger will fade. One day I will know how this ends. One day I will be on the other side.

Just not today. Today is for walking, one step in front of the other, trying not to trip.

Pressed but not crushed. Persecuted, not abandoned. Struck down, but not destroyed.

Never that.

On God and Loss

The text came hard and fast and early, just before my world would explode into a frenzy of action, kids needing a walk to school, work needing doing. And though the noise did not falter, because my boys brushed teeth and scooted chairs and closed doors and opened them again and turned plates and zipped backpacks and asked what was for breakfast, my world grew silent on the heels of a monster. On the heels of death.

It is not so very long ago that my brother and his wife had to say goodbye to twin boys, on Father's Day that year, and now here we are, in the smack dab middle of the holidays, in the sacred stretch of waiting in expectation, in the Advent season when a girl-child awaited a divine baby, and there is another baby lost.

Another baby lost. Another little girl we will not know this side of glory. This one a niece.

My sister-in-law wrote words in those early morning hours, about a labor they couldn't stop, about the pains she thought were just normal pains, because they were two days from the safe-er date, and to have it all go wrong now, to have a baby come and not be saved NOW would be too cruel, too awful, too hard to bear.

And yet she came, two days before her make-it date.

Callie Diane, a cousin and niece for whom my boys and I have prayed every night since knowing of her tiny life inside my sister-in-law's womb, praying without ceasing after that first text came flying across the miles almost seven weeks ago: "My water broke." We had hoped and begged and cried and begged and whispered and begged. And the God who has the power to give and take away chose miracle after miracle, keeping this baby safe and healthy and alive for forty-seven days in a womb with no water.

And then, when they were almost there, he chose to take away.

What kind of God?

///

I got the call about my beloved grandmother one morning just after feeding my toddler. Memaw had always been special to me, the rock who took us in when my mother left my father and needed a place to climb back to her feet, a generous woman who opened the doors of her home, again, the summer I finished my freshman year of college, because she knew Houston had greater job opportunities than my hometown. And she did it again the summer I graduated college and worked for the *Houston Chronicle* while I waited for a wedding that would bind me to San Antonio.

She'd had a stroke, my mother said. She had fallen.

Something had pierced her belly and no one knew it. No one thought to check for internal bleeding before they injected blood thinners into her body. No one checked after all that, either, and she stretched out on a hospital bed and lost every ounce of blood to a wound no one could see.

She died.

And then they brought her back to life, once they'd realized their mistake, pumping massive units of blood into her, and she woke up. She lived. Except she didn't live. Not really. She could breathe, yes. Sort of. She could see and hear and process, mostly. We didn't really know how much of her was left. What we did know is that we were not ready to let her go. She had only lived seventy-four years of life, after all, not nearly enough.

I drove all that way to the hospital where she lay, and I went into the room, by myself, to see her. She was strapped to a machine that measured the rhythmic beating of her heart and the oxygen level blown from a mask and her blood pressure, which was always the problem—but not here, when medicine was injected into veins instead of forgotten in a pillbox she never opened. I looked at the tubes coming out of her, every which way, and at the mask covering half her face, and I bent over her and took her hand, and she looked right at me, and I didn't even have to try. The words just came pouring out, words to a God who could work miracles, a God who could heal, a God who is

Jehovah Rapha.

I called his name. I prayed for half an hour. I squeezed her hand. And when I was done, I asked her a question.

"You won't give up, will you, Memaw?" I said.

And this woman who hadn't talked since her fall, said, "No."

"You're going to be okay," I said.

"Yes," she said.

"You're going to live," I said.

"Yes," she said.

They didn't think she would talk again. There was so much brain damage, so much that couldn't be repaired with just the giving of blood. It would have to be the giving of a brain, because this one was ruined by three minutes, maybe more, without oxygen and three strokes counted up over a lifetime. And yet she was talking.

It wasn't time for her death, Jehovah Rapha said. And I *believed* him.

I kissed her cheek, knocking the mask a little askew, and then I fixed it, and after that I said, "I'll be back to see you soon," because I knew she would be up and about, defying all the doctors' predictions, before I could make the drive to this place again. Hope walked out the door with me, warming all the places fear had chilled.

She would make it. Of course she would. Because we had prayed. Because he had answered.

And then she didn't. She got worse and worse and

worse, and it wasn't a peaceful dying, either, it was a rough, hold-on kind of dying. It was traumatic and hard and undignified, and I couldn't believe it. I could not believe that I had been stupid enough to think that Jehovah Rapha would answer this prayer, ever.

My grandmother did not live, though we had prayed and believed.

What kind of God?

///

This morning I stood in the kitchen, listening to my boys talk about their dreams last night, and I didn't hear a single word they were saying, because all I could think about was this baby, my niece, and my brother and sister-in-law and how in the world I could tell my boys that the baby for whom we'd prayed so earnestly had died anyway.

And then my sister-in-law texted a picture of her perfect little girl with bruises on her face where they had tried to resuscitate her. I could not look at it without crying. Because she was perfect and because she was my niece and because *she should have lived.*

My boys didn't notice, too intent on eating their breakfast, so I turned to them, and I laid it out all blunt and angry, because what did it matter about dreams when there was a brother and a woman who is a sister reeling from the death of yet another child?

"You know the baby we prayed for, your little cousin Aunt Sarah was carrying?" I said. They all looked at me and nodded. "She was born yesterday. And she died."

My voice broke right in the middle of it, because who ever, ever, ever wants to say those ugly, awful, heartbreaking words about a tiny little miracle? I couldn't say more. I could only shake my head and turn away.

And the second-oldest said, "Just like our sister," and the table got all quiet.

They did not know their sister. But they know of her. They know of the girl we prayed for and wanted and imagined in the lineup of our family because she was made to be there. They know of the girl who died.

This pack of boys, who hear the comments people make everywhere we go ("You were trying for a girl, weren't you?" and "All boys for you? No girls?" and "It's too bad you didn't get a daughter in all of those boys"), they may not understand just how cruel the taking is, but they do know that there is someone missing. Someone they might have loved. Someone who might have lived, if God had said so.

There are babies who die and babies who never come and lovers shot down in the streets and friends who take their lives and cities that are bombed bloody and fathers who fall off the wagon and grandmothers who die in a way we will never, ever forget, writhing and shaking on a bed. There are prayers answered and prayers left unheard, it seems, and we are powerless to change any of it. There is only one who holds this power.

What kind of God?

///

We didn't expect to lose a baby. No one ever does, of course, but for us, it had always come easy, the conceiving, the carrying, the bearing. And when we learned of our fourth baby, we did not consider that it would be any different. Except it was, and suddenly I was in a place I never even knew existed, a silent place of grieving for a baby we never had the opportunity to know but who lived in our home all the same.

For a whole year her big brother had been praying for a sister. It's unclear why exactly he wanted a sister, just that he was tired of welcoming brother after brother. He was so excited to know that we were going to add another baby to the family, because he knew this one would be his sister. And he was right.

I took him with me to my second prenatal appointment, so he could hear the heartbeat I'd heard at the first one. And there was no heartbeat.

He sat in a corner of the doctor's office while the nurse practitioner searched and then the obstetrician came in and searched, and he was still there, waiting to hear the rhythm, when my OB said, "These things happen sometimes" and I collapsed into a soggy pile of sobs.

He was there to walk me out of the doctor's office and he was there to try to cheer me up, though there was no cheering up from a tragedy like this one. He was there to tell his daddy, "The baby lost her heartbeat" when I could not say the words. He was only four.

It wasn't until later that we found out she was a daughter. It wasn't until later that I met her in my dreams. It wasn't until later that the silent cry slid deep into my heart, to be brought out in a great wave of rage another day, another day that was four years, five months and three days after that one. Another day that was yesterday, when another little girl died.

What kind of God?

///

They did everything they could, she said. All those doctors. All those men of science. They did EVERYTHING there was to do so they could keep a baby alive, raise her heart rhythm above fifty beats per minute, but in the end, all they could really do was place my niece in her mama's arms and let her die. And so, in the same hospital where, eighteen months ago, she watched her twin boys die, she held another baby, another promised one, another prayed-for one, and watched the breath stop in a tiny mouth and watched the color fade from a tiny face and watched the life leak from a tiny body. One pound, seven ounces, twelve-and-a-half inches of miracle, a little girl who had fought so hard to stay alive, even after she came into the world too many weeks too early.

She was blue and beautiful and alive, for only moments, and then she was forever gone.

What kind of God?

They did everything they could. It was up to God.

"My rainbow. My answered prayer. Washed away so quickly," my sister-in-law wrote later that day.

"I'm truly sorry my body failed you, couldn't keep you safe," she wrote this morning.

Three perfect babies denied them. Three babies covered in prayer and longing and hope. Three babies carried halfway, moving within, holding on to heartbeats, and then, at the very moment their parents finally got to hold them, they breathed their last breath. Given and then immediately taken.

WHAT KIND OF GOD?

I am angry. So very angry. It's not fair. It's not fair that it comes so easily for some and so difficult for others, this thing we call life, this thing that is really, mostly, like an every-day living war. It's not fair that some get to have so many kids and some have so few or none at all. It's not fair that every day my sister-in-law, a neonatal nurse, sees girls twisting in labor, girls who never wanted babies in the first place, girls who will give those babies away in the end, and she will deliver them and hold them and place them in the arms of a mother who does not love them like she would, and she will remember the weight of her own gone ones.

It's just not fair.

No one ever said it would be easy, but no one said it would be this hard, either. No one said it would be this torturous, this excruciating, this traumatic. No one ever said how hard it would be to hold on to hope, because God works all things for good, and God doesn't give us more than we can handle, and through God all things are possible.

Except he doesn't. And he does. And it's not.

At least that's what it feels like in a place like this one.

And of course I know the truth, deep down, because I grew up on truth, but that doesn't change the truth of moments like these, either, when it feels like the only thing that is left for us is a tiny little god who doesn't care one bit about the tender, broken hearts of his people. Who waves his cruel little hand at tragedy and doles it out flippantly like it's something everyone should want. Who thought it would be just the right plan to play with my brother and sister-in-law for forty-seven days after her water broke, let them hope that making it this far meant they'd make it all the way this time, and then take a prayed-for, desperate-for baby two days from the we-made-it point.

What kind of God is this?

I know what kind of God he feels like right now. But I also know that hope and faith and love are mysterious things. They hold on even in the strongest of winds, even in the deepest of waters, even in the fiercest of fires. I have been down to the bottom of the world, and I have stood back up again. I have been blasted into a pile of ash, and my dry bones have found life again.

I don't really have the answers. Sometimes there are no answers, no matter how hard we search to find them. There are no answers to why one baby survives and another doesn't. There are no answers to why some get everything they want and some only get asphalt and hunger and shame. There are no answers to why some die and others live.

It's not easy to see and hear and feel God in a place as ruined as this one. It doesn't seem like we will ever see or hear or feel him again.

But I know he is still here. I know he is peering over my shoulder, watching my every word, reading the texts I send to my beautiful sister-in-law, aiming the light so it shimmers around the corners of this dark room, still. Forging the way through and out and to the other side so it opens up like a morning glory.

So it ends its twisting, jagged path right in the lap of love. Eventually.

On Family Trees that Look Like Stumps

A month ago we drove the three-hour trip to my hometown, my boys and husband and me packed up in our Honda Odyssey, trying not to drive one another crazy before we got where we were going.

We were traveling for a special occasion. My mom had rented the same facility where my husband and I handed out gifts to our parents and our bridesmaids and groomsmen the evening before our wedding. This time she rented it for a goodbye, because cancer is eating away her stepmother.

She walked into the room, and we all tried not to be shocked by all the weight she'd lost. I tried not to cry when I hugged her thin neck. I tried not to turn away when those wrinkles gathered around her mouth and eyes as she watched my boys chase each other around the room that had held so much happiness eleven years ago. I tried to watch instead. I tried to soak it in. I tried to feel and remember and know.

And then my grandpa cleared his throat and everyone got quiet and he talked about the birth of my mom and her sister and their baby brother and how it was all joy in the midst of pain, because there was a marriage falling apart yet three children to show for the crumbling.

He had married this dying woman, my step-grandmother, thirty-five years ago. And even though their story is full of pain and heartache and loss, I know, too, that it is full of victory. People had transformed and lives had changed.

Beauty hid in all the shadows.

///

When I was nine years old, my gifted and talented class was assigned a family tree project. We needed to collect information about our family culture and values and stories and explore all the family limbs sitting green on a sturdy trunk.

It was one of the hardest projects I've ever done, because I tried to connect all those names—Papaw with Memaw, except they'd divorced and he'd remarried Granny, and then there was the other side, Grandma and Pop, only he wasn't my real grandpa because she'd divorced, too, and married him before I was even born. And then my parents divorced and my dad remarried, and there were half brothers and a half sister, and I didn't even know what to do with all of it. It was so confusing, too disordered, too dysfunctional. The branches of my family tree were all stunted and tangled and torn, and what was left looked more like a gnarled stump than anything that could possibly grow and bloom.

In a family that could not brag of a perfect tree, what could we really know of love and hope and life? What could we really know of family?

///

What we know of family were raucous Christmas dinners with aunts and uncles and cousins, when grownups would sit around a table playing Trivial Pursuit while the children begged a turn, too, even though the questions didn't make a bit of sense to them most of the time (sometimes we got lucky on the music questions). What we know of family was a grandmother taking in three grandchildren and a grown daughter for a year after a divorce left them broke and broken, a grandmother who had spent her years cooking dinner for her own children and now spent another one cooking dinner for three more children who were not exactly grateful, because they hated being there, without their dad, without a space of their own, without the assurance that this arrangement wouldn't last forever. What we know of family was a grandma and grandpa putting aside the bitter taste of divorce so they could sit in the audience while a graduate delivered her speech, to try to make her forget that one empty seat.

We knew hard, and we knew messy, and we knew awkward, but we also knew devotion.

Family doesn't always look neat and clean. Sometimes it looks like a great-grandfather who beat his wife and an older half-brother with a prison time record and thieves and drunkards and addicts. There are secrets, and sometimes they are ugly and shameful. But it is in these shadow places that we learn what it means to forgive and accept and love.

This is where we learn to be family.

///

He showed up at our door for meet-the-kids-night with two large pepperoni pizzas, and I knew this was the man my mother would marry. He was younger than she was, with a three-year-old boy, but he looked at me and my sister and my brother like we mattered. Like we were somebody. Like we could put back together two broken worlds. Like he didn't know if we could do it for sure, but he would damn well try.

They married on a sunny day in April. My sister and I wore dresses his aunt made. I sang a love song. My brother held the hand of our new step-brother, trying to get him to stand still during the vow-making and the ring exchanging and the kissing.

And then the man who had vowed to be our father the day he married our mother went to work.

He took us in like we were his own, because that's what he'd promised my mother he'd do. He sat, bored out of his mind, at my volleyball games and band concerts and all the track meets he could possibly make. He whistled that loud whistle after my brother's trumpet solo at the football

We Count it All Joy

game, because it really was amazing. He drove me to college and stood outside my dorm with my mother, trying not to show his emotions when we all said goodbye.

He knocked down all those walls in the hearts of three children, and he took his place inside, so he was the one who walked my sister and me down the aisles on our wedding days. He was the one who didn't miss a baby's birth. He was the one our hearts called Dad.

And maybe it took a while, and maybe we didn't make it easy, and maybe it wasn't the least bit perfect (because what remarriage is?) but he stuck around, and that made all the difference in the world.

It was hard and disappointing, that divorce piece, but *this* piece, the putting-back-together piece, has been wildly beautiful.

///

In the room with my Papaw and Granny, who is the only grandmother I have left now, even though she's a step and won't be around much longer if the cancer has anything to say about it, sat my beautiful aunt, by the side of a man who is not my uncle. She bears the scars of a thirty-year marriage, of being left for another, of spending three years flailing, trying to make sense of a divorce and what comes after. She has lived a story like her mother did, like her sister did, and yet…

And yet there is this man who popped the question to ring in a New Year with surprise and joy. She said yes and pulled those last limbs from the tree.

There is something I have learned in all of this history, and it is this: Family trees are good and lovely and wonderful, and it's comforting to take shade beneath their limbs when the day gets too hot. But a family stump offers something, too.

A stump offers a sitting place, a thinking place, a resting place that cannot be disturbed or shaken by high winds or heavy water or the changing seasons. This is the gift of a broken family. But the gift-receiving is up to us.

You see, we can choose to be victims of our broken stump of a family. Or we can choose to let that stump be our victory.

I don't know who I might have been if my family had stayed intact all those years ago, if I had come from generations of healthy marriages and unbroken people. But I can say that this stump of a family, who it has made me, who it has made all these people I love most, is enchantingly lovely.

One day my boys will ask about this tangled family stump. And I will tell them its stories with all the gratefulness a heart can possibly feel.

On that say-goodbye day last month, my stump beckoned me. It said, *Sit and stay a while.*

Visit.

Love.

Appreciate.

And I did, until it was only my wildlings and their daddy and the ones they call Nonny and Poppy left in the room.

On Wishing for a Different Life

It's been a day of chores and dragging kids around with us, and everything has taken three times as long as it normally would, because kids are whining for water and dragging their feet and hiding between racks of clothes so we can't find them for one heart-stopping moment they think is funny.

It's only one hour into the madness when those words march their way to my mind: *I wish my life were different.*

I wish my life were different.

The realization that it's true, at least in this moment, is hard to swallow.

///

When I was a little girl, I knew exactly what I wanted to be: an author and a singer. And also, somewhat less likely, the first woman president of the United States.

I had plans, big, big dreams for my life, about writing books and performing music to adoring fans and running political campaigns, and I did not plan on marriage or kids slowing me down.

I stumbled into my last year of college, well on my way to living my author dream (the president dream had fizzled out somewhere around the time I took my first government class). While many college seniors find themselves nearly overcome with insecurity and fear of the future, I was ready for my launch into the world—except for the growing ache to meet the man who would share my successful life with me.

And then I met him.

It was raining the fall evening we stood in a tiny historical church, with all our friends and family watching, and said "I do."

More than two years we were married—going on dates any time we wanted, taking spontaneous shopping trips whenever the mood struck us, booking an anniversary getaway without much ado—before we started talking about children. We said yes and then we said no, back and forth, because we didn't know what we were doing, and we were pretty sure it would completely change our entire lives, and what if we weren't ready yet?

Is anyone ever ready for children?

And then there was that first pregnancy test and another one ten seconds later, then two more of them, just to be sure.

I told him in the car, right after picking him up from work. He stared, open-mouthed, and didn't say a word. I burst into tears.

///

They stay in the car with their daddy while I grocery shop alone, because already there's been too much noise and my head is aching and this needs to be done quickly, at least quicker than kids will allow it to be done. I roam through the aisles packing a cart, watching all those other mothers out with their one or two children, the way their carts are about one-fourth as full as mine, and I nearly laugh. I don't even remember a time when I bought so little food for a week's eating.

I find myself wondering what it would be like to be them, with a grocery bill that didn't compete with a housing bill, with a day of errands that didn't mean losing one of five little ones every other minute, with a home that didn't need a mom's voice magnified by a megaphone to be heard over all the noise.

And this line of thinking leads me to how I desperately need a vacation from all these children—a whole year-long one, it feels like—how no parent can survive without help. Mostly, though, this line of thinking leads me somewhere familiar, to a place where I wish I could be a better mom— the kind of mom who doesn't wish her life were different, the kind of mom who doesn't sometimes regret having children, the kind of mom who is always content and always happy with the way her life moves and shifts around a tribe of boys.

The truth is, I don't always feel happy being a mom.
///
Before the first one was even on our radar, I landed a job at one of the largest newspapers in Texas, reporting for

the community section. I covered everything from fashion shows and city council meetings to musicians and artists who lived fascinating lives.

Two years in I moved to a political beat, covering elections and special events in the state capital, while, in the meantime, working on a series about women and substance abuse that I thought might have a fighting chance for a Pulitzer.

I never finished the series, though, because of a pregnancy test.

Instead, I gave up the job and chose another that was more flexible and family-friendly and less demanding, all the while hoping I could, in my spare time, finish that addiction series—because it was an important story to tell. But when you're a mama who works, there's not really any spare time. So I set it aside until it was too old to pick back up without starting over from scratch. I set aside my Pulitzer dream. I set aside my book writing. I set aside anything extra, because all I could manage was work and home and baby.

My dreams would just have to wait until he was older. I thought it would be easy then.

But it didn't happen that way, because there was his brother, two years later, and another boy fourteen months later and twins eighteen months after that.

///

It's dinnertime, and my head is keeping time with my

heart, and there's still dinner to be made. Always, always, always dinner.

And after dinner is cleanup and family time that will be spent cleaning tonight, because boys have destroyed our house today, and then we'll run the crazy race toward bedtime.

I feel the dread of it all in my shoulders and my neck and the pit of my stomach, so I bite out every word that needs saying:

Just get in your seats and wait.

Please stop asking for things because I'm working as fast as I can.

I can't take the screaming and whining and crying.

Stop. Stop. Please stop.

And when it's all said and done I don't feel even remotely close to a good mom anymore. All I can think is this: I wish they were different. I wish I were different. I wish my life were different.

These words gorge a hole straight to my heart's dusty corners, where all those dreams folded in on themselves years ago.

Sometimes it feels impossible to be a mom. Sometimes none of it has turned out like we expected. Would I have done things differently if I had known this day was coming?

I could have been a successful writer. I could have been a president. I could have been anything, and instead I am

Mama.

///

I had my five, and they had their none.

It didn't feel fair, sitting across the table from my sister who waited for a child while I had five. It didn't feel fair, shaking out a good cry for my brother and sister-in-law, who prayed and begged for a child and got two born too soon and then watched them die, while I had my five still living. It didn't feel fair, the way they longed for my life while I wondered what had ever possessed me to choose it.

They could barely make it through a day without tears for their child longing, and I could barely make it through a day without tears for my child-having, because this mothering business is hard, hard, hard work. Maybe I underestimated how difficult it would actually be raising five children born in five years. Maybe I overestimated my ability to mother well all the days required of me. Maybe my expectations were the problem all along.

///

The boys are wild tonight, even though there were no naps. The library is a wreck just like their rooms, all this destruction after less than an hour of unsupervised playing-upstairs time. I can't take it. The thought that throws itself against the tender spot above my eyes is, *When is this must-supervise-them-at-all-hours-of-the-day going to end?*

I'm picking up hangers from the floor for the second

time in ten minutes when their daddy comes in and I send words flying into rain and wind and storm.

We shouldn't have had so many children.

He looks at me, surprised, because I've never said anything like this before, even through all those blurry-eyed nights with twins and the potty training mishaps and the months before school could offer us the tiniest of breaks. And it's not that I don't love my children, or that I would be able to give any one of them away after knowing and delighting in who they are, or that I could even imagine what my life would be without them.

It's just that sometimes it's all so overwhelming and chaotic and unmanageable that I can only imagine it would somehow be easier.

But the thing is, having children does not mean I gave up who I am. This is the truth whispering in my heart even as I free those words that have plagued me all day. No. Having children means that I am becoming more of who I was created to be.

There are times I am so overwhelmed with it all that my heart can find no word but *Please*, and there are times when discipline issues knock out my feet from under me so I can only hear *Help* pounding through my chest, and then there are times when I look at them and I see—really, really see. The oldest reading to his "twinsies" and the second one helping his daddy make pizza and the middle one showing me his favorite monster shirt that looks so cute on him I think I could cry, and the overwhelm blasts differently, thick and warm and love-filled.

My sons are scraping away the places in me that don't belong.

My sons grab my need for control and shred it in their piano-banging, picture-drawing, sword-fighting hands. My sons teach me to forgive and let go and love wholly and fully and completely. My sons keep me tethered tight to a God who is much bigger than five little boys and their destruction and their constant, never-ending needs.

Sure, I could have marched toward Washington or autographed books that printed in the millions or accepted a Pulitzer prize, but my sons make that could-have-been life look dim compared to this shining-five-times-brighter one. And no moment or two or two hundred like the ones I've had today would ever, ever change that truth.

Tonight, when lights are dim and boys are settled in beds, I climb in next to the four-year-old for our snuggle time, and he tells me a story of his tiny little pink owl he spent fifteen minutes picking out at one of the stops today because he had a couple of dollars to spend.

And that smile says everything.

This is the best life for me, by far.

On Public School

Another of them starts school this week, taking that first step on a thirteen-year journey, and there are two of them now, away from my influence seven hours of every weekday, and I can feel the fear of it catching in the back of my throat.

It happens every year, just like this, and every year I have to fight off that failure-feeling because I cannot be a homeschool mom.

I could protect them from so much. I could drill those values so deeply in their hearts they'd never get them back out. I could speak life into their lives all the time, instead of relying on a behavior chart to teach them who they should be. I could control their friends and their food and their learning and their choices and their decisions and their opportunities and their playground interactions and their exercise routines and their literature reading and their library visits and the soap they wash their hands with and the way people around them talk.

My heart has begun its jagged beating, again.

I wish. I wish. I wish.

///

My first day of kindergarten I walked into a classroom

not much bigger than a dorm room, lit by lamps and a back wall of windows. Mrs. Spinks hung all those alphabet balloons, an apple with an A, a penguin with a P, a zebra with a Z, in every corner of the room, and she pointed, three times a day, to the checkered carpet sitting in the center of the room, where we'd learn our letters and their sounds, even those of us who already knew how to read because our mama was a librarian and our ten-months-older brother had come home every day from his kindergarten year and taught us everything he knew.

My brother had refused to sit in that neat circle on a checkered carpet the year before, but I did everything I was told, eager to please in any way I could.

Just after lunch, the room transformed into a blue-carpeted mat, because we all stretched out our nap pads and Mrs. Spinks would turn on that big noisy fan and all my classmates would sleep around me while I stared, wide awake, at those bubble letters, creating elaborate stories in my mind that linked them all, the zebras and the penguins and the apples and everything in between.

In that room we colored and slept and sat at desks facing a chalkboard with no computer anywhere in sight, and we were such a small town everybody's parents knew everybody else's parents, and we, the students, had already known each other for years.

It was safe.

///

Two years ago, when my oldest started school, the whole family walked him into a room with desks facing each other in pods and math sums arranged on posters and stacks and stacks of handwriting pages he and his classmates would work through by the end of the year, because all those five-year-olds, or most of them, already knew their letters and only needed some extra practice writing.

My boy didn't seem to notice that day the proximity of those desks, how they never gave a student one minute to be alone, but he would in unexplainable ways later, when he'd yell at his brothers to leave him alone and when he'd cry about things he never cried about and when he'd fall asleep on our bed, even though he hadn't napped since he'd turned four.

I wondered, a hundred times, a thousand, if we had made the right choice.

But I worked a job, and we depended on my income, and that made homeschool a can't-do option, and all those littler ones still at home, four of them, made it an even greater impossibility.

In those first days, I did what most first-time-public-school mothers do—I wrote a note to his teacher to explain my boy's little quirks, the way he prefers to take off his shoes after playing outside because he wants his toes to breathe, how he enjoys teaching himself and reads animal encyclopedias and Harry Potter and environmental guides, how he loves hard and strong and wild like a tornado, an often-overwhelming thing for those who are loved, as he would likely love his teacher.

I wanted her to know him the way I did, and I wanted her to accept all those quirks, all those strong-willed bones that hold a hard line in his body, and love him anyway.

And then we walked our beloved one to school and left him there at a seat that bore his name. I hoped all the way home that he would feel as safe as I did when I was a five-year-old girl in a world I had never known. But you can't make a teacher love a child, and sometimes the only safe place you can give him is his home-place.

I would learn that later, and it would drive another spear in my heart.

///

The kindergarteners in my small-town school shared a playground with everyone in school, just like we shared a cafeteria with one lunch period and a gym with a small stage so it doubled as an auditorium.

Our playground didn't look at all like the playgrounds of today. A merry-go-round and a metal slide on one side, three seesaws edging it, and, in its middle, a bank of swings and above-ground culverts and cut-in-half tractor tires painted sky blue and electric orange and pale yellow, set upright for climbing onto and under. A cement slab waited across the street for P.E. class, but we weren't allowed to cross the street during recess.

That first day I stayed far away from the seesaws and the merry-go-round and the tires. I stuck to the swings, because it was what I knew, and I could kick my feet high and feel like I was flying for that half-hour of free time twice a day.

It was safe.

But as the weeks wore on, I watched friends climb through the above-ground culverts, where spiders hung from cement tops and snakes might be hiding in the grass patches between them. I thought if they could do it, I could, too.

A friend and I hid in one of those culverts during recess one day, and there was a boy, years older than us, standing just to the side of it. I knew by his scratchy voice who he was, a big boy who rode the bus home with my brother and me.

Hey, Fatton, he yelled so everyone on the playground could hear. I peered out of the culvert. He was pointing at my brother, just across the way, climbing onto a seesaw with a friend small and thin. *You're too fat for that, Fatton.*

He wasn't fat, my brother, just solid, built like a football player, but the name would stick all through elementary school, and that boy would be the torturer, and he would drag along with him other boys, boys who went to church with us and boys whose moms knew our mom and boys who came from good homes with a mom and dad who loved them and tried to raise them right. They would all tease with a pleasure I could never understand.

That day I learned that school could be a not-so-safe place, one that could take a last name, Patton, and turn it into Fatton because someone thought it was funny and didn't think through what it might do to whoever was on the other end of it.

///

It's not so different, this world where my sons will walk to school and sit in a classroom and play on a playground. And yet it's so very different.

Bullies existed back when I was a girl, but we knew each other's parents and we knew each other and we didn't hide behind technology and computer screens and entertainment that existed outside of real relationships with real people.

We knew how to look our tormentors in the eye. We knew how to see that their mom was dying of some disease doctors didn't know how to cure and how his dad worked too much and never spent time with him and how they were afraid of our brains and our dreams because they somehow believed ours stole something from their own.

My boys, though, are coming of age in a world that values performance over empathy, that holds up competitions as the only way to achieve, that mandates boys walk angry and wounded and shut down, because to show emotion is to be a lesser man, and they don't know how to express their deepest hurts outside of the violence they see everywhere, in games, in movies, in their homes.

They will live in a school world where men can walk in and shoot five- and six-year-olds, where boys carry knives in the front pocket of their backpacks, where bullies on the playgrounds can rip holes in a heart faster than a mama can mend.

How does a mama keep her sweet boys safe in a dangerous place like this? How does a mama make sure her boys keep holding tight to who they are in a culture that thrives on pointing out who they aren't? How does a mama breathe on a day like today?

///

All the kids braved the monkey bars back when I was a girl, even though they were so high off the ground even an adult had to swing across instead of walking themselves across.

There was a day when I watched a boy, my brother's best friend, get halfway across and then drop, his body twisting all the way to the ground, his hand trapped beneath him so it cracked in three jagged pieces. I watched him turn pale as the teacher on duty led him away. He returned two days later with his hand and wrist wrapped in a white cast, ready for signatures.

I watched a friend brave the big metal slide that burned our behinds raw when the sun was out, and she slid all the way down, her legs squealing for her, and then her bare-skinned thighs stuck to the bottom so she had to throw herself off, and the throwing knocked her off balance so she fell on her face and lost two front teeth. I watched her cry herself bloody as she ran off to find help.

And then there was another day, when we all sat in a cafeteria where the smell of chicken noodle soup shifted and turned and stretched, and I sat down with my friends and dipped my two cheese rolls in broth and ate them first, and then I heard the yelling, and there was my brother, turning blue, and Mr. Tegler, the district speech therapist, behind him, lifting and squeezing until that bone flew out of my brother's throat and he sucked air like it was all he'd ever wanted to do. I watched his face whiten in the relief of breathing again when he thought he never would.

My brother could have died. He could have died. He could have died. That's what I remember thinking minutes, hours, days later. He could have died.

In a place this unsafe, it could happen to anyone.

///

My sons could die. My sons could die. My sons could die. Every step closer to the school, I feel those weights closing in. How do I protect their dreams from death? How do I protect their hearts from death? How do I protect their bodies from death?

I could drive myself crazy with all these questions I cannot answer.

I can twist and turn under that not-really-a-decision public school decision, and I can let the guilt nip my heels all the way through the halls to those classrooms, and I can feel the burden hanging my neck and dragging my feet and choke-holding my heart.

Or.

Or I can let them go, let them take this first step out of my arms, because there will be so many more that must be made after this. I can loosen my hold to their own capable selves, to a God who knows them better than I know them myself.

I am a mama, and I will always hold them tight, in arms or in my ragged raw, letting-go heart, but there is Another who holds them, too, and as hard as this letting go is, I must remember they will be caught. They will be held. They will be loved.

I can keep them hidden and safe, or I can let them go to shine like noon in a world of midnight. I can keep them within the bounds of my home and my carefully controlled community and my list of approved friends, or I can let them go to stand on legs of their own and live out values and missions and love in their own way.

I can teach them to crawl in my safe-zone perimeter, or I can let them go fly.

I want to be brave enough to let them fly.

So I take the first step. I swallow hard, and I kiss them both goodbye, and I whisper those words into their ears, *Remember who you are. Strong. Courageous. Kind. And most of all my son,* and then I walk the sidewalk back home, with three more who wait for this flying.

On the Secret to Marriage

We are talking of the future and business plans and all these topics that beckon anxiety from its hiding place, because we're in such a precarious position with so many unknowns. He is asking for hope and trust and certainty, and I can't give it in light of all those years when plans didn't work out like we thought they would and disappointment came loping in like a stray dog. What if this new plan ends the same way all the others did?

His eyes, wild and furious, tell me I've said exactly the wrong words at exactly the wrong time in exactly the wrong way.

But there are children in the car, so he bites his lip and stares out the front window, and he will not be able to say what he wants to say until we get home and feed kids and put them down for their naps, because there is not a moment alone until we do.

We let the silence speak for us.

My head starts turning it over and over, how maybe I shouldn't have said what I did, but, God, I'm so tired of arguing about the same old things and having the same old conversations about the same old dilemma. All those years adding up to tired brought words to my mouth without so much as a second thought. That's not an excuse. Simply a reality. A confession, maybe.

You can't take back words. So these words sit and fester in both our hearts, waiting for boys to sleep so we can fight the ugly wrinkles back into smooth.

///

It took him a while to convince me to spend the rest of my life with him. There were two other possibilities, a boy destined for politics and another for professional baseball, when he came along. My future husband came crashing through both their plans with his black curls and blue eyes and a voice that could soothe me into love when he talked, but especially when he sang.

The problem wasn't that he was the tiniest bit dorky or that he wasn't very good with money or that he wasn't even sure what he wanted to be when he grew up. The problem was mostly that when he looked at me, he really *looked* at me. He really saw. He really knew in the deepest ways a person could know. It unsettled me. I was so good at hiding feelings and pretending that life's hard punches hadn't even winded me and constructing this identity of a laid-back girl who had her whole life figured out. I worked so hard to lock away those secret places. And here was a boy-man dismantling all the walls and staring into the bare places and shouting that what he saw—all the ugliness curled inside a little girl's heart—was actually beautiful.

I wasn't ready for that, and I wasn't sure he was The

One, and I couldn't really tell if this was love or a timid kind of hope.

Mostly, though, I was afraid of the greatness he saw in me.

I held him at arms' length for as long as I could, and then I crumbled. He slipped a ring on my finger, and we stepped into forever.

///

He still knows in the deepest ways a person can know. When I say there's nothing wrong in that specific tone of voice, he knows it means there really is; I'm just not ready to talk about it yet. When I say I had a hard time writing today, he knows it's because it's the last day of the month and tomorrow I'll have to sit in front of a computer and try to reconcile our budget. When I say I need to go to Wednesday night church, he knows it's because I need time to myself, without anyone bothering me or trying to get my attention or asking me for something. He just knows.

He knows how I'll respond or react before I do. He knows what I'm feeling before I can even articulate the words. He knows my motivations and my fears and my shaky hope and my annoying realism and the way I tie my shoes with two bunny ears and how I'll feel about my son's playground experience today and the words I'll say about the one who won't leave us alone at bedtime and what I think about the book I'll pull open tonight.

Living together, scraping against each other's edges,

sharpening the iron strength of another for as long as we have, means that you really, really know someone in the deepest places. You know how they're feeling and how they see the world today and what they need at just the right times. It can feel scary to be known this way. When we are known, we have no place to hide. When we are known, we are vulnerable.

When we know, we see all their vulnerable. This knowing can turn cruel, and sometimes it does, taking its anger-shot at the exact place it will hurt the most.

That's all a part of the marriage story.

///

I had never met anyone quite like him before. When I was sick, he stayed by my side, holding my hair as I bent over the toilet or lying beside me while I burned up with fever or carrying me down fifteen stairs after I broke my foot.

When I spoke, he listened and heard. When I dreamed, he believed those dreams were possible. When I cried, he did not run away. When I raged, he met the fire.

For the early years of our marriage, I lived with a ball of black in my heart. It spoke of abandonment and fear and a bottomless well of insecurity. Sometimes that ball flew out of my mouth and wrapped around words. Sometimes it took off the screen door of my heart and nailed up a cedar one instead. Sometimes it aimed its arrow and sent hurt into my husband's heart.

Every single time he forgave. He never held grudges or threatened leaving or wondered if he might do better for himself somewhere else. Instead, he stood solid against all those years until I began to soften. And then he loved me more tenderly, more profoundly, more wholly.

I have still never met anyone quite like him.

///

A fight like this one is not the first in the nearly twelve years we've been married. Of course it isn't. Because we're human. We're imperfect. We're selfish. We speak without thinking. And when you've been married this long, you know what all the words say, but you also learn what the silences between the words say.

In every marriage there come seasons of waking up on a different page in a different book, feeling more like strangers who fight than friends who talk. We have had days, weeks, months of tension and push-and-pull and butting heads and asking forgiveness, and every single time—every single time—we have walked out of that shaky season stronger than we walked in.

Every single time.

We fought and we disliked and we raged and we cried and we opened our umbrellas and we hid in ditches during the storms that sometimes only dumped rain but sometimes felt like a Category 5 tornado, and through it all we fought for love.

We all say words we don't mean to the ones we love.

And then we all have the privilege of stepping outside ourselves and meeting the other person's hurt with humility and remorse.

The secret to saving a marriage is not avoiding all the conflicts. The secret is letting go of our pride. Saying we're sorry. Choosing love over winning. Forgiving.

Sometimes, when we are entrenched in those days and weeks and months of conflict, when it feels like we can get nothing right and we can't say a word without arguing, it can feel like conflict tells the whole story of our marriage. But if we look closely enough, we'll see.

Forgiveness after forgiveness, *this* is the whole story of a marriage.

And so, today, while boys eat their lunch, I follow my husband up the stairs and I wrap my arms around him and speak my apology into his ear. Tears mix on both our cheeks, but that salty water is really sweet. So sweet.

Because it tells the real story of a marriage. The real story of partnership. The real story of love.

On Mothering

She turns sixty this week.

I have known her for just more than half of those years, and in the same way she has watched me grow from infant to toddler to teenager to adult with infants and toddlers of my own, so I have watched her grow.

I have watched those black-brown eyes she got from her half-Choctaw great-grandmother, the same ones she gave to me, soften with the forgiveness of years spent working on it. I have watched the mouth she gave my sister smile without the weight of worry more than I ever did as a kid. I have watched her skin wrinkle into beauty lines that speak of wisdom and bravery and joy and a fierce determination that pulled her through all the hell of her past so she stands, today, mostly victorious.

A couple of weeks ago, we pulled off a surprise birthday party for her, and she walked through a closed door into a party room crammed full of close friends and family who love her. She laughed about having no idea of these plans, because she thought everyone had forgotten she had a birthday coming up at all and had begun planning her own celebration, with a tinge of sadness that she had to plan her own. We went right along with her plans so she wouldn't know our secret, and then we gathered a week early and shouted our surprise and laughed at her shock.

I don't know if she knows it or not, but the surprise we yelled said much more than that one word.

How could someone forget a remarkable woman like you? it said.

I get to call her Mama.

///

My first memory of her is bright yellow, with orange and pink and blue around the edges, like a brilliant sunrise. She is reading a book to us. She was always reading books to us, because this is what librarians do for their children. She had a deep love for words, and she wanted to make sure her children loved them, too.

It was in that same house, not long after my first memory, that I remember watching my dad disappear on his motorcycle, and I ran into the house and threw myself onto the bed I shared with my sister, sobbing in my four-year-old hysterical way because I didn't know when I would see him again.

She knelt by my side for as long as it took, stroking my back while I cried. She didn't try telling me it would be all right. She didn't try telling me he would be back soon. She didn't try telling me he was leaving for our good.

I would learn later it was because she didn't know any of those answers herself. She just hoped. And prayed. And went on with her life, caring for the three of us on her own.

She is the strongest woman I know.

///

She knelt by my side for another crying, too.

It was the first time I'd had a boyfriend. We dated for a month, or maybe two, and I was in love with that tan and those blue eyes framed by thick black lashes and the way he threw a baseball from the mound. And then he decided to date someone his own age, since I was two years younger, and I was heartbroken, sobbing once more into a pillow on my daybed.

She didn't knock, just came on through without a word and knelt beside me and stroked my back. She didn't tell me there would be others or that I would probably be glad for this breakup someday or that I was only fifteen. She sat there, and after a long, long time, she told me stories from her own falling-in-love days, about the boy who had called into a radio station her junior year and dedicated a love song to her, and it was too much too soon; and about the brother of a friend she'd had a crush on since grade school and how he never liked her back; and about the others who didn't seem quite right for her. And by the end of it, I knew I wasn't the only girl who'd ever had my heart broken like this.

She left my room, and I sat there in the growing dark, thinking about how this woman so beautiful and amazing had handed her heart to a man, a husband, who had broken it in ways I couldn't even imagine.

She is the greatest woman I know.

///

I was four or five that morning we were headed to church. We had just stepped out the front door when my mom said, *Get in the car, kids. Be quiet, but be quick.* Or something like that.

My brother and sister and I did as we were told without asking any questions, probably for the first time ever. We locked the car doors behind us. There was danger in her voice.

We watched her disappear into the house and come back with a gardening hoe. She rattled the branch of one of the trees that stood like a canopy over our yard, and something fell to the ground, something striped and long and thick. It writhed on the ground.

She started hacking, in her Sunday dress, chopping like her life depended on it. She saved us from snakes we couldn't see that morning.

She hunted other snakes, too.

The ulcers and sorrow and anger that chased my brother after my parents' divorce—she hunted those snakes on her knees, praying ceaselessly for him. A boyfriend who asked me to marry him early on, one who held a look she knew too well—she hunted that snake with boundaries and limitations and refusals, knowing what would eventually happen: he would stray and I would leave for good (she was right). The money worries that followed us like an unwanted dog, because she never could quite make ends meet with three growing kids—she hunted that snake with a school librarian job on the weekdays and a candy-stocker job at the local store on the weekends.

There were some snakes she could not see, like the ones that waited for my sister in the dark closets of a friend's house, and the ones that burrowed not-enough holes all through my own heart, and the ones that wrapped my brother tight and hard and closed him to the men around him who might have taught him how to be a man. But she tried with every single day of her life.

She is the bravest woman I know.

///

In sixth grade I signed up for band. In seventh grade I added volleyball and basketball and track, because I didn't know what I most wanted to do. My mom let me throw myself into all of them.

She worked all day and cleaned house in the afternoons and then sat an evening away in the stands, cheering and clapping and paying attention even on the nights I sat the bench.

In high school, there was marching band and state competitions and volleyball and track and softball and tennis, and I wonder how many of those she wanted to miss. But she never did. She watched me direct the band as a drum major my junior and senior year, and she watched me braid the hair of my teammates in the year I had to sit volleyball out because of a knee surgery, and she drove all the way to a town forty miles away on her only day off to watch me run the 300-meter hurdles, even though I purposely scratched the event because I was so terrified of the humiliation of tripping and falling.

She was there the day I made second chair in the state band, even though I wanted first. She was there the day I ran the 800-meter run for the first time, even though I gassed out by the end of the first lap, since I'd only ever run the 400, and I came in dead last. She was there the day I stood on a graduation stage in my silver robe, shaking through my valedictorian speech while all eyes were on me and the maroon hair I'd dyed the night before as some kind of statement I've forgotten now.

She let me be who I was, and she stuck around to watch the failures and the victories so she could love me through every one.

She is the kindest woman I know.

///

There was a night we walked in late at home from my brother's fifth-grade basketball game, and the answering machine was blinking. My dad had planned to come to the game but never showed, so, thinking it was him, my mother pressed the button. An unfamiliar voice said her name. And then the voice said, *I just thought you should know your husband's girlfriend is three months pregnant.*

We stood there, unmoving, unblinking. All the air had been sucked from the room, and not one of us could breathe anymore.

And then my mother said those words in a clear, strong voice: *It's just a prank call. It's not true.*

My mother could lie when it mattered.

And even though we wondered, deep down, if those words were truth or lie, we loved her more for the cover-up.

She didn't say words like that often, only when she knew we needed them, like the time we waited on a call, all of us strung tight with the waiting and wondering and hoping. *Of course he'll call,* she said, even though it took him three years. *Your milk will come in,* she said after I had my first baby, when I stumbled down the stairs teary-eyed and exhausted and too disappointed to speak, even though it never did. *They'll be out in no time,* she said the day my twins were born and nurses whisked them off to neonatal intensive care and I cried and cried and cried, even though it took them twenty agonizing days.

She is the most loving woman I know.

///

She is a piece of my history I am proud to call my own. I have watched her blossom into a loving grandmother, doting on all these boys (*It's the same feeling I had when you kids were born,* she said after the first one slid into the world). And now that I am a mother, I know the courage and perseverance and determination it takes to be a good one, and I am so thankful she carried me in her womb and carried me through my growing-up years and carries me still into my mothering ones.

This woman, who kept every one of my earliest stories in a cardboard box under her bed, is the best mother I have ever known. I am who I am because of who she is. She is a hero, a warrior with battle wounds and a bruised purple heart and a legacy of love that saved the lives of three people, and so many more. It is in her heroism that she has taught me all about how to be the greatest mother.

Great mothering does not live in being the greatest housekeeper or the greatest lunch-maker or the greatest provider or even the greatest teacher or discipliner.

Great mothering lives in being the biggest fan.

It means letting children be who they are instead of trying to change them to be who we want them to be. It means guiding them gently in the way they should go instead of beating them toward our way with words or hands. It means staying present in the failures and the victories and all the places in between.

It means being the person they most want to be, because we love and honor and cherish and teach and hold and accept.

This was my mother's gift to me.

This was my mother's gift to the world.

On Fathers

We all gathered on the same two acres where my sister and brother and I grew up, though the house we lived in for seven years no longer sits on the land. Another marks its place instead: wider, longer, newer.

Fajita meat smoked on the island in the middle of the kitchen. A bowl of my mom's potato salad hugged the edge of the counter, a metal spoon jutting out of it. A cake, frosted in white, covered in candy mustaches, bleeding red along the sides, waited to be cut.

It said, "Happy Father's Day."

I'm not a cake person, but my eyes would catch on those words every time I passed by the island. *Happy Father's Day*, it said. Happy Father's Day.

All day long I felt something pinching at the corners of my existence. All day long I shoved it back down where it belonged, hidden and safe in a heart that had come to terms with this, truly. All day long I tried to forget about my rocky relationship with the word "father."

But it's not something a fatherless child can so easily forget.

///

My memories of my father, especially the first ones, are

vague and hazy and uneven. I remember looking up to him and marveling at how tall he was, like a giant. I remember watching everything he did with awe and adoration, like he was the very definition of a hero. I remember how he smiled, his eyes crinkling up in a way that made you want to do whatever you could do to elicit another, because they were so few and far between.

I remember hands that would hold me when crossing a road, so I would be safe, and hands that would redden my skin in successive smacks for crying harder when he threatened to give me something to cry about. I remember tall glasses of milk with butter biscuits and the mess of a kitchen my mom would have to clean up after my father decided to cook. I remember a bright yellow truck and swimming in a murky lake and words that could sting worse than his hands.

I remember standing beneath a cover of trees, the wind pulling at my dress, whipping it against my knees and calves, while he climbed on the back of his motorcycle. I asked him when he would be back. He said nothing, only smiled, blew me a kiss, and drove away. I watched him until I could not see that motorcycle anymore, until I could not see him anymore.

And then I remember gone.

///

At my mom's house, the fathers stood around outside, talking over a barbecue pit. They chased little ones inside, saving them from plummeting off a couch. They bent over a game of croquet and taught boys how to putt.

Midway through the day, I ambled outside and saw my brother-in-law, leaning into a tire swing, helping my niece onto it. He pushed her in gentle circles, and she giggled. She asked him to push her again, and he did, this time higher. Her face changed, and her hands wrapped tighter around the rope. She made a little noise, startled by the feel of flying higher.

He heard the noise and stopped her, reassuring her she was safe. She climbed down and ran off across the wide yard. His eyes followed her, and, when her face grew too red and sweaty, he carried her inside for a drink of cold water.

I watched, and I wondered.

I wondered what it would have been like to have a dad who noticed. A dad who noticed that your face changed almost imperceptibly, because you were trying hard to be brave, but the truth was you were scared. I wondered what it would have been like to have a dad tell you it was okay to be afraid, that he still loved you even though. I wondered what it would have been like to have a dad who saw your thirst and met it.

My dad noticed the shortcomings and the mistakes and the journal he once took it upon himself to read. He told us all the ways he would have raised us differently if he'd been the one to keep us, instead of our mom, who, he said, coddled us too much. He saw our thirst and called it complaining. Neediness. Weakness.

Ridiculous. Inconvenient. Too much.

The words needled into my skin, becoming three completely new ones: Not. Good. Enough.

///

It took him a long time to come back, but he did. He came back and then he went away again, and then he came back and went away again. After a year of his being gone, my mom told us we were moving.

To Ohio, she said.

To be together, she said.

Like a real family, she said.

We cried and protested, and when the crying and protesting didn't work, we despaired and hated. We didn't want to leave our friends, our home, our security. We'd never even been out of the state of Texas, but we went in the end. We had no other choice. Being a real family was too alluring.

My mom settled us into the largest house we'd had, or at least that's how my memory tells it, even though I can't remember the rooms all that clearly, because a veil dropped over my memory that year, as if my life had been a candlelit movie set until a move to Ohio turned it into a darkened theater, with only flashes of clarity.

But what didn't happen in the Promised Land was my father coming home. We weren't a family. Nothing changed.

My father's absence in that year carved a jagged hole in my heart. I tried to be the best I could be, so he would come home. I tried to make the best grades, tried to have all the right friends, tried to be perfect, tried to be less of an inconvenience, tried to prove I was worthy of love. But nothing I did could bring him home.

We left Ohio with failure whipping across our backs, and I would work harder in the years that came after, always trying to prove I was somebody. Somebody great, somebody noteworthy, somebody who deserved a loving father who stuck around.

The harder I worked, the larger the hole grew and the larger the hole grew, the harder I worked. It was a cycle that could not be tamed.

I fell fast and furious into it.

///

I was a seventh grader when my stepdad showed up at the front door with two large pizzas and met us for the first time. He was a young blue-eyed buzz-cut-haired man who treated my mom like she was something special, and as much as we loved that about him, we could not forgive him, at the time, for taking my father's place. And we made it hard on him.

We shouted our disrespect, and we fought with our hands and our hearts and our words, and we told him we didn't want him to live with us, never ever ever. We did everything we could think to do to make sure that our father's space was untouched. Saved, if you will. Because our father might one day return.

It's hard for a kid to let go of that dream. It's hard for a kid to let another man step into the place of one who should have loved them unconditionally, recklessly, forever and always just because they shared his blood and genes and the long legs and thin lips and straight hair.

But my stepdad stuck around. He fought for our hearts. He picked up all the pieces my father left and said we could be his. We could be loved. We could be good enough.

My stepdad walked me down the aisle, and he sat in the waiting room the day all my sons were born, and he calls my sons his grandsons, even though they share none of his blood. He has shown me what it means to be a father. It does not mean abandonment and forgetting birthdays and wishing out loud in the hearing of a kid, that the kid could be different.

It means putting a heart back together with Duct tape and calling it spectacular anyway.

///

My husband is one of the most hands-on fathers I know. He cares for our children for half a day every day while I hole up and write. He plays with them, he raises them, he speaks life into them. I watch him sometimes with a mixture of love and awe, because I never knew that a father could be like that. So present. So forgiving. So involved and heroic and wonderful.

I never knew a father's love could be so spectacularly life-changing—not just for the ones who are the recipients of it, but for the ones who are watching it unfold around them.

A father, in my world, had only ever picked up and left, moving on to another family—one that was better, easier, more worth the work of sticking around. But healing crept into my heart, watching my husband. Not just because he was a phenomenal father but also because he messed up.

He messed up. My father messed up. We all mess up.

A father has a tough job, this being a hero to the ones who look to him for truth and love and identity. Some fathers aren't up for the task. Some are. Some try. Some don't so much. Some step into the role and play it for all it's worth. Some are too afraid to even toe it.

And some? They just don't even know where to start.

///

Father's Day. It's not an easy day for me. I always feel a bit guilty that I only really call my father once a year, on Father's Day. Sometimes I don't even do that. Sometimes it's just a text. Sometimes the whole day goes by and I'm so busy with my husband and boys that I forget to even text.

Part of the problem, see, is that my father is not the first person I think of on father's day. I think of the man who stuck around when the going got hard and I turned into a contrary teenager. I think of the man who stood there, stoic, when I called him an idiot because he wouldn't let me go see my boyfriend. I think of the man who spun me around the dance floor during the father-daughter dance the day I got married.

Father's Day isn't always a simple day in the lives of the fatherless ones. Some of us have blood fathers who gave up and called it quits, and that damaged something deep inside, told us we weren't worthy of the effort it takes to be a dad. Some of us have fathers who left in other ways, like death or suicide or an accident that rendered him inaccessible to us. Some of us never even knew our dads.

We were hurt by our dads. We still carry the scars. Maybe we haven't quite forgiven them.

And so when it comes time to celebrate dads, we say, oh, well, it's just another day in my life, because I never really had a dad anyway.

But there is something I have learned in the years between that vulnerable eleven-year-old and this woman I am today, and it is this: Dads come in many different shapes and sizes, and the ones we think of on Father's Day aren't always the ones who scientifically contributed one half of who we are.

The fathers of our heart look like teachers and coaches and friends' dads and stepdads and fathers-in-law and mentors. They look like the ones who step into our lives when others step out. They shape us the same as any dad should, even though they didn't have to. They fill us. They rebuild us. They are dads.

And so, for Father's Day, I choose to thank all those men who step into the lives of the fatherless ones and teach little boys how to be men and little girls how to be loved. Thank you for your presence. Thank you for your generosity. Thank you for your love.

Happy Father's Day to all the fathers of my heart.

On the Missing Chairs at Thanksgiving

In a few days some of my favorite people will gather around my living room table, and we will talk over turkey and heap a plate with mashed potatoes and gravy and pretend we're trying to decide between apple or chocolate pie when we know we've already planned to take a slice of both. Some of us will be missing this year because of in-law dinners and lives too many states away, but a small group will sit and celebrate the sacred family tradition that is Thanksgiving.

We will start that meal with a prayer, like we always do, and the four-year-old will grin into my face, because he's so excited his Nonny and Poppy are here; and the five-year-old will try hard to close his eyes but won't be able to help that roving gaze, because he's always loved a food spread like this; and the eight-year-old will shift from foot to foot, because his daddy sometimes prays a little too long.

And we will give thanks in our hearts for all we have seen and done in the year stretching between this moment and the last time we all met around a table and a turkey and two pans of green bean casserole.

Love and hope and awe and wonder meet us here.

///

It's hard to know when those first memories of Thanksgiving began. There are flashes of days down through the years, one at a great-uncle's house with woods looming behind it and a long wooden swing hanging from the trees that shadowed his yard and pine needles thick like a spiky carpet on the ground.

There is a great-great grandmother's house, all of us squeezed in the tiny square footage her husband built, where legend had it she slept with a gun under her pillow because she lived alone and the neighborhood had turned a little dangerous for an old woman and she wasn't the least afraid to use it, and I remember the way the kids would sit out on her cement porch and swing or drop pieces of paper or leaves through the little mail slot so it would fall in the middle of her living room, reminding the adults we were still waiting on that food-call.

There is a great-grandmother's house, after the great-great and the great-uncle were gone, and this gathering looked and felt smaller because so many of the older ones had died, and others had drifted away with the dying, and it was only a handful of kids who went out front to play kickball while the adults and my Nana watched a game on her living room television. All the kids missed the false teeth flying out when a referee made a bad call and Nana screeched at the screen, but we heard the laughter of all the adults who witnessed it.

These early memories are raucous and full of children

running in and out of houses, trying not to stick fingers in the pies, and I can still smell that turkey and the fresh bread and those vegetables we didn't even know the names of.

I couldn't explain it then, not in words, but I could feel the thanks that burst from the first bite of food, all the way to the last bite of pie, when we all felt like we might pop and surely wouldn't eat again after this.

There was something simple and special and sacred about those shared days. They courted joy.

///

Thanksgiving Day has lost some of its magic now.

Maybe it's because a job demands work until the very day of thanks. Maybe it's because kids go to school and homework still comes home and schedules still remain the same until Thursday rolls around. Maybe it's because of all who are missing now.

When all those greats were alive we had so many families gathering around so many tables, and now, this year, we have two. There are no more greats around for the little children. Those children's parents are the ones hosting dinners now. There aren't even always aunts and uncles who join in the festivities anymore, because we all have our own lives and our own plans and our own families.

Gone are the days of great aunts and uncles all under the same roof for the same day breaking bread and eating their fill and trying not to notice how everyone looks older this year.

I feel a little sad about this. We used to pack a house on this traditional holiday, and now that holiday demands work and dangles big sales and asks families to cut short the one day a year when they might fall asleep on a couch after eating too much turkey and no one would mind their snoring.

I miss that magic.

///

There is a Thanksgiving that stands out as scary and new and somewhat disappointing. I was nine years old, and we had just moved to Ohio because it was the only way my mom thought we would ever be a family again, since my dad worked in Ohio and our home state of Texas was a long way off. She told us the news a month before summer ended and listened to us cry about leaving our friends, and then she packed us up and we moved into a two-story house in Mansfield, six or so rundown blocks from an elementary school.

We didn't have the money that year to go back home (Texas would always be home) and spend the holiday with my mom's family, who held all my memories of Thanksgiving to date. So we spent the day with my dad's family instead.

My paternal grandmother was a saintly woman. It wasn't her fault that she and my grandfather were the only two I really knew in that group of thirty or so. It wasn't her fault that I had never felt more like an outsider than I did that year. That day.

Cousins who had grown up together, whose names we didn't even know and I can't recall today, played hide and seek in Grandma's travel trailer, and my brother and sister and I stayed out under the trees, raking leaves, because we didn't know them and they didn't know us, and raking leaves at least gave us something to do. So we raked and waited for that screen door to open and let us know it was time to eat and we could finally blame our silence on food.

When they called, we all trampled inside a house that smelled like cabbage.

It was the first time I ever threw up after a Thanksgiving meal.

///

I wonder what my boys will remember of Thanksgiving, this holiday that is not so wild and noisy and crowded as it was in my girlhood because there is only them and a grandma and grandpa and, every other year, an aunt and uncle or two who bring a handful of cousins.

Will they remember these Thanksgiving days as thrilling, with a haze of laughter blurring them into gold? Will they remember adults playing board games and talking until the sun goes down and the whole sky turns dark? Will they remember how eagerly they waited to sit at the "adult" table, wondering every year if this one might be the year they move up past all the babies?

The spread at our Thanksgiving is nothing like it was

for me as a kid, with rows and rows of homemade pies and sweet tea like syrup and a whole table full of steaming food in too-hot-to-touch bowls, but does it still look magical to my sons? Do they feel the people who are missing, all those family members who have come and long gone, or do they see a room-for-more house as full?

Do they notice the lost pieces like I do?

///

Then there was the first Thanksgiving without my maternal grandmother.

She had been there for all of the holidays I could remember but one, short and regal with black and white curls, always quiet in a corner chair so she could observe her family, because she was content simply to be in the same room with all of them.

She died in early February the year I only had one baby, and no one was thinking of Thanksgiving the day we gathered inside a church and mourned our great loss in gushing sobs until we had headaches and swollen eyes and a whole pile of crumpled tissues stuffed in the bottom of our purses.

No one thought of Thanksgiving when it came around, either. It came and went, without my aunts and uncles or any of the people left who might have carried on this sacred tradition of Thanksgiving Dinner. We didn't carry on.

That year I hosted a small family gathering at my

house, where my brother and sister and mom and stepdad and husband and only one baby boy sat down at a table set for six, with a highchair hanging on the end. It was the smallest family gathering we'd ever seen for Thanksgiving, because the one who held all the rest of us together was gone.

I didn't know then that it would become the new standard for a family with a missing piece.

///

How much do we lose in this place of smaller family gatherings? I don't really know.

As much as I grieve my family's loss of larger gatherings, I cannot separate myself from something else I have learned in my adult years, something I never had to know as a child. In our world, there exist those with no family left and those who can't physically travel to their family and those who have long been rejected by their family, and what about these on a day like this?

There are those who don't eat half as well as we do on Thanksgiving, or any other day, and what about them? How do we even celebrate family around the abundant spread of a table when there are those who are lost and hungry and alone?

Maybe the answer to those spaces left in our home by the ones who are gone waits right outside our doors, at the house beside ours or the one behind the park or the street corner down the way, where the man selling newspapers works just another day of his life. Maybe we become family for those who have none.

My table will be full for Thanksgiving this year, but there is room still for more. I want to find them. I want to know them. I want to bring them home, into the fold of light and love and laughter like I have known.

It's Thanksgiving, and we will eat and we will reminisce and we will give thanks for all we have and the people we love and the whole last year's beauty. But that is not The End of Thanksgiving. Because true Thanksgiving becomes thanks-living, and thanks-living means thanks-giving to the world, to all those who need what we have, be it food or presence or simply an invitation.

So this Thanksgiving, I see the hollows and the spaces, and I thank God for them, because, even now, they are waiting to be filled.

Someone is waiting to be filled.

On the Firstborn Son

I watch my boy from where I sit, his back curved a bit while his head hangs over the Star Wars book he's reading, and I marvel at how his brow is missing the soft spot between eye and forehead, how his face has thinned out of the baby cheeks and chin, how his mouth moves in silent speaking while he is so lost in the world of a book. My boy is no more a baby, but he will always be my baby.

In two days he will celebrate eight years since his birth day, that day when my body bore down and his body tore through, a day when boy became first son and girl-woman became Mama.

"I know how I was made, Mama," he said last year on his day, when I set a birthday brownie-cupcake in front of him. "God took a piece of your heart and made me."

He has a gift with words and truth and insight. He saw it exactly right. All my children are a piece of my heart walking and jumping and racing around outside my body, and it's scary and risky and agonizing to let loose those heart strings so they can learn to walk on their own, but this is how we learn to really live.

The love between a mama and her boy is wide and deep and strong enough to knock us all flat.

What I have learned of love, what I have learned of grace and forgiveness and joy, what I have learned of life, I could not have foretold that chilly night in November, four days before Thanksgiving that year.

I have never been the same.

///

He slid into the world late, when the sky was pitch black, and it was a mostly perfect, by-the-books birth, with a perfect, rosy-cheeked baby and a perfect love all the way from the beginning. And then they released him to two young parents who didn't know what to do with a seven-pound, fifteen-ounce baby except let him steal our hearts.

We laid him in a Peter Rabbit bassinet that first night, after reading him a bedtime story, and then his daddy and I found sleep to the sound of a new being breathing just beside our bed.

I woke before he did for that early, early morning feeding, and he was still sleeping soundly, but the darkness, all above his bassinet, was moving, swirling, like something lived in the dark, something sinister and sharp and full of a death that did not steal breath but something greater—life.

I picked up my baby boy and held him in my arms, and I prayed while he fed, and when he was done I held him and prayed some more, and when my arms got too tired to hold him anymore, I laid him in the bassinet, but I didn't stop praying until the first shards of light reached right through my window, until that twirling dark lifted from the corners of the room, until the fingers that fought to reach an innocent baby's form had completely disappeared.

It was my first all-night vigil for this boy whose name means *Jehovah has heard*.

It would not be my last.

///

Just a few weeks ago, I tossed and turned and prayed and listened and tried hard to find my way out of a confusion too dark to see through.

My boy had spent three days in school suspension for choosing to act outside of who he is, and I was sick to my stomach and sick at heart, trying desperately to crawl my way toward understanding. I tried to find the words that came so easily all those years ago, at my first all-night vigil, but the only words that would come sounded more like: *Help. Please.* Over and over and over again.

He is too big now to hold in my arms all night, but I held him in my heart.

It was all mere weeks after announcing we were expecting boy number six, when all those people filled a comment box with words: *I guess you're just really good at raising boys.* But here was my firstborn, the boy who first stole my heart, proving them all wrong.

There was more he had to teach me here, this child who has always been strong-willed and incredibly creative and a wild hurricane of love.

Sometimes our parenting journey takes us right up

against the places where it feels like we don't know what we're doing and it feels like we are not enough or we were never enough or we will never be enough and it feels like we are flailing in a midnight where all the stars have gone out. Sometimes we need to stall here and stay a while.

Our children will show us the way back out.

///

The day before Thanksgiving that birth year we raced him to a children's ER, because he hadn't produced a wet or dirty diaper in twelve hours. *Your milk will come in*, my mother had told me the day we brought him home and I could not even pump an ounce and could not say for sure that my baby was eating anything at all.

I sat in the emergency room, holding my four-day-old, watching the way he slept so peacefully even though my whole body shook with the knowing that he could have died from his dehydration.

They called us back and woke him with a needle, trying to find a tiny vein so they could hydrate him again. He cried and screamed and writhed on a table while they poked the bottom of his foot and then his arm and then another hand and then, after all the others slid out of their grasp, the largest vein in his forehead.

I watched my baby, hooked up to a hydration drip, and I noticed the way those glassy eyes stared at the nurse whose face hung over him, how he searched the room for his mama when he realized the face wasn't the right one, and I cried and cried and could not stop crying. My body had failed him already, four days in. I had failed him already, four days in.

It would take all the days after for him to set me straight. I had not failed him, not really, because I was still his mama, and that was all he needed.

I loved him and he loved me and that was simple, but it was enough.

///

Love would always be enough.

Even on the days when strong will met frustration. Even on the days we yelled and said those words we didn't mean. Even on the days we walked bruised and bloodied and broken for all the mistakes we made. Every mistake, every failure, every less-than-ideal moment was remaking me.

It was not just this boy who slid from a womb eight years ago. It was me, too.

A child, this child, and all his little brothers living inside my home, have led me deeper into the way. They have drawn me closer to the Way. So it is not just his birthday we will celebrate in two days. It is my birth-anew day, too.

As hard as this journey has been, the ways he has taken apart all our parenting philosophies and rearranged them completely, the times we have walked, shaking, off the ledge into a boy-world—I would not trade it for all the easy and predictable certainty in the world.

Sure, there have been days when he has raged and I have thrown my rage to meet his and we both bled through tears and words and wonderings, but I would not give away those days, those opportunities he has given me to practice asking forgiveness and limp toward a better vision for parenting, because they have taught me about humility and grace and freedom. Sure, I used to watch the two-year-old nursery where all those kids sat on their designated seats while my boy climbed onto the one he'd already chosen before the teachers pointed out a different one, and I would wonder how the other kids could be so obedient and well-behaved and calm, but I would not wish a perfectly obedient, minds-all-the-time child in his place, because he has taught me acceptance and joy and what it's like to surrender to earth-shaking belly laughter. Sure, there would be days when he walked out the door and threw back those words, *I'm going to run away*, and I wanted to let him, but the truth is I would chase him down to the ends of the earth, because he has taught me how to love in all the hardest places, and I don't want to stop learning. Ever.

The only time I ever considered my boy easy was when he was a baby, but I'm glad. What he has taught me in his challenge whispers truth about a mama's strength, so much greater than she knows, and a mama's hope, so much wider than she can see, and a mama's great love, so much deeper than she could ever understand.

Thank God he is alive. Thank God he is mine.

On Being a Working Mom

"Do you work?"

We're sitting at the pool. The boys are swimming with their daddy, but I'm sitting out with my four-month-old and my still-broken-but-almost-healed foot. A woman has just counted up all my children and laughed about "all boys." The youngest smiles, because he's joyful like that.

"Yes," I say. "I'm an author."

"Oh," she says, and it's not a condescending sound, more of a surprise-mixed-with-wonder sound.

So I break the ice. "I need my work so I stay sane," I say, and we spend the next ten minutes laughing about how we can only handle so much and how work feels like a vacation sometimes and how we are both better mothers for our out-of-the-home pursuit.

The truth is, my out-of-the-home pursuit is not just for me. It's also for my family. For our finances. My family needs my contribution to stay above water, so even if I did want to stay home, I couldn't. I wasn't always okay with this reality.

///

Just before my first son was born, I took a job producing a newspaper for one of the Methodist conferences in Texas. It didn't pay a whole lot, but it was steady and it took care of the electric bill and the water bill and the Internet bill and the grocery needs and the gas expenses.

And then my son crashed into our lives and the whole world turned upside down, and I just wanted to spend all my time with him. I didn't care about promotions, didn't care about accolades, didn't care about anything except being present with my amazing little boy so I wouldn't miss a single thing.

Except my husband didn't make enough money to pay our bills on his own, and we needed two incomes. So I had to work. I had to keep my job.

I arranged a compromise with my boss: I would work part of the day in the office and part of the day at home so I could still hang out with my boy. I had the best of both worlds, watching my son in the morning while working on the pieces of my job that didn't require complete and uninterrupted concentration and letting my husband hang out with him while I went to the office in the afternoons. We made our trade-off work. We divided chores. We supported each other in every way we could.

And yet something still felt wrong. Something still felt suffocating. I thought it was because I was still working. I was still a mom who was still working, and I was not made to work. I was made to raise my child.

A bitter ball settled in my throat.

///

We are mothers. We can convince ourselves that the best thing in the whole world would be to stay at home with our babies and raise them to love reading and teach them how to write in journals and shape them into people we actually want to hang out with when they're older. This is what mothers are supposed to do, after all. It's our duty. Our calling. Our inheritance.

Sometimes it's possible to find a way to stay at home, if we look hard enough. Sometimes it's not, because health insurance premiums went up too high and the cost of food has increased outrageously and the car needs some unexpected repairs we didn't anticipate in the budget we made last month. And when the finances fall short and we realize we can't stay at home because more than one income is necessary to care for our family, we can sometimes get shockingly bitter about it.

If only our circumstances were different. If only our husbands had chosen a different career. If only he made more money.

If only…

It's not easy to pull ourselves back out of this if-only pit.

///

Six months ago I was laid off from the job I'd had for nearly nine years. We found out about the layoff a few months in advance, so I spent the last months there feeling sad and out of sorts and terribly unmotivated. I wanted to finish well, but how do you finish well when someone doesn't want you?

In the meantime, I was searching for a new job, because my income was still necessary for our family. The old bitterness was rising up to meet me.

There was a day, close to Christmas, when I came home from work especially drained and sad and maybe a little angry, because the bad news had been repeated in different terms. I could practically see the walls shaking as I walked up to my door. I put the key in the lock, and I could already hear the world falling apart into hysterical laughter. Then I opened the door, and there was my husband, in the middle of all my boys, except the one I still carried, doing "The Robot."

"Dance party!" he shouted above the music.

I just stood in the doorway watching my boys giggle and rearrange their daddy, watching them all dance, watching those faces that glowed with such happiness I could hardly handle it. An overwhelming wave of gratitude knocked all the bitterness from its stronghold.

They might have missed this, I thought. They might have missed sharing such a sacred time with their daddy if I weren't a working mother.

They might have missed.

It was the first time I really felt glad that I had worked all these years. Glad that my income was necessary to raise my growing boys. Glad that my husband had *this* time with them.

Just exceedingly glad.

///

We don't have to feel guilty or bitter or angry about working outside the home, because our working gives a gift to our husbands. It gives them the opportunity to be present with their children, to play with their children, to share in the raising responsibility of their children that will change lives forever.

We don't have to feel guilty. We don't have to feel shamed. We don't have to feel bitter.

In our working outside the home, in our sharing the household responsibilities, in our taking both hands off the wheel for a moment in time, we are letting our husbands be intentional dads, letting them take their important place beside us in this journey of training up a child in the way he should go. That's the picture I got, all those months ago, when I walked into my house with bitterness in my hands and saw why the walls were shaking.

It's not unusual, today, to see dads who stay home with their children. And while many shake their heads and say it's just another way women are taking over the workforce, I can't help but think that a generation of involved dads is so much better than a generation of disinterested dads. It means we get a whole generation of children who grow up with present dads, not absent ones. It means we get boys and girls who know who they are because their dad has spoken it into their lives with not only words but also time. It means we get little ones who recognize how valuable they are to their moms *and* their dads and, by extension, the world.

I can't help but believe this can only be good.

So today I am thankful for my split-down-the-middle day. I am grateful that I get to work. Most of all, I am glad that my husband has the privilege of speaking into the lives of his children in ways that mean life and freedom and love.

I'll go to work any day for that.

On Trading Recordings for Memories

It's the last week of school, and I am a weeping mess. It's not a sad weeping, really. It's a bittersweet weeping, a proud weeping, because every step they take on this road that is education and growing up and moving on is another step they take out of my home.

Those heartstrings tied to them want to pull tighter, shelter them from the heartache I know is coming, because it always does. I want to protect them and hold them and keep them.

Mostly I want to keep them. Keep them small. Keep them safe. Keep them here. And yet this week has reminded me that keeping them is not something I can do.

Two days ago I watched my eight-year-old walk the stage for his second grade completion ceremony, where he got the "Artful Artist" award. Yesterday I watched my six-year-old sing and sign and accept the "Best Reader" award during his kindergarten completion program. Today I watched them both dance their way into summer.

Or I tried. It was hard to find a window between hands and arms holding video cameras and smartphones and iPads where I could actually see them. I ducked and turned and moved, and everywhere I went there was another device recording the moment. I had to squint and tilt my head just the right way to see my sons.

At first I felt angry. Annoyed. Because I was a parent, too, and I deserved to see my sons bust a move just like the next person did.

And then I remembered: It wasn't so long ago that I did the same.

///

Two years ago, when my first son was a kindergartener, I stood in the throng of parents and tried to take a video of him dancing, because his daddy wasn't able to come and his daddy needed to see, but mostly because I wanted to keep the memory forever and ever and ever. The whole time my Canon 7D kept slipping away from him because I was trying to watch him in person, not on a screen, so the video isn't even a very good one.

I watched him stand on his tiptoes waiting for the music to begin and I watched him strike that last pose and I watched him walk away with a grin I could barely make out on the screen of the camera. I could not see that grin shine. I missed the way he made a goofy face at his brothers in the crowd and made them all burst out laughing, because I was so intent on getting the perfect shot. I missed the way his feet fairly flew off the blacktop because he was so excited that he'd nailed the dance. I missed looking into his eyes and letting him see the pride that shouted from mine.

I missed. And to this day, I wish I had the vision in my memory store more than I had the video on my computer's memory store.

When my boy got home from school, he didn't even ask to see the video. He didn't care that there was one. He only talked about when he had done that jump move and did I see him throw some break-dancing into the free form section? And I had to admit, at least to myself, that no, I hadn't seen it, because I was too busy trying to capture video.

I missed.

///

We miss something in these moments we work so hard to preserve. We miss the living of them.

It takes us a while to see it, because we are the first generation of parents growing up in a world of technology that puts access to video at our fingertips, without having to set up the perfect shot or figure out the best lighting or get as close as we possibly can. We have zoom lenses and autofocus and cameras that can take five pictures per second.

And everything feels so necessary. I know. I felt it this year.

I purposely decided, before each of the school events, that I would not pull out a video camera this year. But when the second graders walked across the stage for their completion certificates and awards and the principal announced that the center aisle of the cafeteria was reserved for parents taking video and pictures of their kids, I wanted to get up. And when my son stood with his teacher and turned to the center aisle and no one was there, I felt like I had let him down. Like I had lost an opportunity. Like I had willingly given up recording a significant moment. But I just waved crazily from the back of the cafeteria and called his name and let that grin of his slide all the way down into the deepest places of my heart.

You see, our kids don't have to know that we are recording their every step and capturing their every accomplishment and putting it all into a folder they won't really care about when they're eighteen. They just need to know we're there. Watching. Enjoying. Marveling. It's hard to watch and enjoy and marvel with a phone between us and every special moment. Sure, we may get to savor it later, but what are we missing right now, in this moment here?

There are some things pictures can't capture.

The excited glow of his eyes. The way his smile lights up the whole room. How he grins even wider, if possible, when he catches your eyes and not just the camera's eyes.

I understand how we can get caught up with every significant moment and want to keep it. Keep them. I know what it's like to feel like you probably should order a class picture and those individual school shots, even though you take a billion better ones at home. I know how a yearbook in elementary school can feel necessary, because how will they remember if we don't find a way to preserve those memories?

The thing is, they don't really need our help remembering what's important.

///

My kindergarten year is hazy in my mind, but I remember balloon letters hanging from a ceiling and a gather-together rug in the middle of the room and a claw-foot bathtub in the corner where we took turns reading for pleasure. I remember blue mats on the floor and lying down too close to a girl who picked my chicken pox scab while I was sleeping and made a scar in the middle of my forehead. I remember pronouncing island like is-land and how Mrs. Spinks corrected me. I remember a playground with metal seesaws and above-ground culverts painted yellow and tractor tires cut in half. I remember losing a tooth in a Flintstone push-up popsicle and my brother choking on a chicken bone, back when the cafeteria chicken noodle soup was made from real, bones-included chicken, and the first time I slid down the metal slide in shorts and burned the backside of my legs.

My mom didn't have to capture any of those moments for me to remember them.

There is something magical about remembering our pasts the way our minds want to remember them. That kindergarten reading bathtub probably wasn't as pretty as I remember. That metal slide probably wasn't as tall (or safe) as I remember. The cafeteria and gym and schoolyard probably weren't as large as I remember.

And part of me is glad a video doesn't exist to prove my memory wrong.

///

Memories are so much more than seeing. They are hearing and feeling and smelling and tasting, too, and a video can only catch two of those. Our memories can catch them all.

I record so much of my kids' lives. When they do something funny. When they wear something cute. When they sing one of their original songs or choreograph an amazing dance or write a play and perform it for us in our living room. I record because I want to remember.

But could I remember without the help? Will I remember how he moved his hands in that funky way during "Uptown Funk" without a video camera preserving it forever? Will I remember the hilarious poses he struck during the freeform part of the dance? Will I remember the way my other son tipped his head and made his body so fluid and waved his hands at just the right times during "Surfin' USA"?

I'd sure like to try—because I want to be present in the moment. Right here. Right now. Looking at them with both my eyes open. I want my boys to know what it means to be fully present in a moment, to soak it up and let our memories do their work.

"Are you disappointed that we didn't get a video of your dance?" I ask my eight-year-old when he gets home from school today.

"No," he says. He grins. "I saw you dancing along."

He knows the truth of it.

A mama can't dance when she's holding a camera.

On Expecting Another Boy

I walk into the dim-lit room, my hopes opening the door for me.

This whole experience has been different—the sickness, the carrying, the exhaustion, the weight gain (almost none at all)—and I caught myself thinking in these days before knowing the gender of the baby I carry, *It's a girl. Surely it's a girl.* And now comes this day my suspicions will be confirmed, and I wait in the light of a screen to hear, my hopes sitting softly on my chest, because even though I've said out loud that gender doesn't matter, this one does.

This one, the last one, matters.

This baby, of course, would be our girl. We knew it, so we tried again. We said, *One more.*

My doctor checks the heartbeat and all those other pieces and asks, *You sure you want to know?*

And yes, of course I do, because I plan to shop on the way home for her first dress and a headband to match.

Another boy, she says, and my heart drops all the way to my toes.

This isn't even something we considered, because who in the world ends their family line with six boys and no daughters stretching behind?

The doctor, who has delivered all my boys, faces her computer screen, chuckling about this revelation, and I'm glad she's not looking at me because I'm wiping away tears I can barely feel, and the whole room spins hazy and blurry and suffocating in a way I don't understand, because this is a baby, for God's sake, my baby, and why can't I just be happy about a baby? Why does finding out the gender of this sixth and last child feel like a dream slamming in pieces on the ground, when I know how delightful and charming boys can be and how much they love their mamas and how we already have all the clothes and gear and bedding we could possibly need, if a little worn and ragged after the use of those five who came before?

I say the only words I can find. *Wow. Poor Ben. He's going to be so disappointed.* And what I really mean is: Poor Rachel. She's so disappointed.

Then I walk out that door with my hopes dragging the floor behind me.

///

It's something little girls like me dreamed about growing up, without even knowing we dreamed about it. I saw glimpses of it when I brushed the hair of my dolls or braided it down their backs or cut my sister's hair in a layered bob. Someday I would do this for my daughter, that was the unspoken knowing. I would brush her hair and braid it down her back and trim what needed trimming.

That desire for a one-day daughter showed up early in my little girl life. Maybe it's because I had an amazing mother. Maybe it's because she had an amazing mother, too, a mother she called every few days about something her kids did or some advice she needed or just because she needed to talk to someone who understood her. Maybe it's because of that old picture, five generations of women lined up like stair-steps, me at the tallest top.

I wanted a daughter to put in that picture. I wanted a daughter to sit in my lap and play dolls with, if she enjoyed playing with dolls. I wanted a daughter who would call me on the phone every few days to tell me about something her kids had done.

I've wanted a daughter since before I could even voice my want. So I took that pregnancy test for my second baby, years ago, and the day it turned positive, I went shopping for girl clothes.

It made sense, at the time: one boy and one girl. And then the sonogram told another story, so I packed away all those girl clothes and tucked away the name we chose, because I knew there would be another opportunity. And there was, number three and then twins. But they were all boys and those carefully chosen little-girl clothes remained in a box, still waiting for a daughter who did not come.

///

It's only a quick trip at the store. I'm not buying many clothes like I would have done if the gender had been different, because we already have enough clothes for a boy. But I need some candy as a consolation prize, since I know how at least two of my sons will react to the news of another brother.

All the way home I don't turn on the radio and I don't sing and I don't talk to anyone on the phone. I just sit and think, trying to reconcile what I've learned today with my expectations.

And then I walk in the door at home, to all the ones who are waiting to hear the news I bring, and I stand behind a camera to film the reveal with their daddy and my mom and only three of the five, because the other two are napping and wouldn't really understand what they're seeing anyway.

They dig in the brown gift bag and pull out the tissue paper, and their daddy tears it apart, and there it is. *Number one brother,* the onesie says.

The oldest starts crying, because he's been waiting for a sister through five of them, and I cry right along with him, behind a camera, pretending I'm really laughing at his reaction.

A brother will be fun, his Nonny says.

No he won't, my son says. *I've had lots of experience.*

Experience that sits a megaphone on the kitchen counters so we can dole out instructions above the constant noise, experience that rips holes in every wall of our home, experience that brings anxiety and a touch of exasperation to the back of my throat when I open a refrigerator that's empty even though we just got groceries three days ago.

I have lots of experience, too. I know what to expect, and though I love my boys with a fierce and undying love, I wanted something different this time.

///

There was a daughter who died.

We didn't get to meet her, but the day of her dying is forever etched in my mind. A doctor's office. A machine that showed no movement of life where there had been before. A hospital that took her from the parts of me that could not let her go.

I always thought there would be another.

I dream of her sometimes—this daughter we named Amarise because it means *given by God*. It wasn't our first-choice name. We didn't want to use the name that still waited for a daughter who lived.

Every now and then she comes to me when I sleep, and she touches my face with one little hand and stares at me with those summer sky eyes, and then she races away, her red curls flying.

I wish we had given her that name we'd saved through all those boys before her.

///

It's in the moments when a friend posts a beautiful picture of her baby girl and the times parents talk about last year's daddy-daughter dance and when moms share about their girls' weekends with their daughters that I feel it the most. It's when I watch my friends with their daughters, the way their mama eyes light up when their daughter walks into the room, the way those little girls hold a piece of their mamas in their eyes and smile and walk.

Everywhere I look in my boys, I see their daddy.

This isn't a bad thing, not at all, because he's a good man and a loving daddy and a doting husband, and if they can be anything like him when they grow up, the world will look much different than it does today. It's just that I don't get to see a piece of me walking around, not really, because they walk like him and talk like him and think like him and play like him and jump like him and fly like him, and I don't always understand their ways or their feelings or their anger like I imagine I would understand the ways of a daughter.

All these days after learning gender, disappointment shoves into my throat every time this new baby boy moves and every time I see that swelling in the mirror and every time I think about another bundle of pure energy racing in a game of indoor tag with his brothers, even though it's against the rules. In my most unguarded moments, I think about how my husband has all these sons to pass along his name and his legacy and a picture of how to be a man, and I will not have this gift, because there is no daughter who needs a name or a legacy or a picture of how to be a woman.

There will never be a daughter.

///

Maybe we shouldn't have done it. Maybe we should have been happy with the five. Maybe we should have adopted. They all think we're crazy anyway, in this society where two children is the national norm. What in the world were we thinking?

These thoughts shake me weeks after learning the gender of our last one, because there is another that attaches to them: *After all, what was the point?*

Guilt chases that one hard.

The day before Father's Day this year, my brother and sister-in-law watched their twin boys slip into the world too early. They watched those boys fight and claw to find air in lungs that had not yet formed, and then, an hour later, they watched them slip into the next world. We have a picture of them, blue babies wrapped in the same blankets all my babies were wrapped in. They couldn't even open their eyes to see their parents before they died.

And then, just a month later, my sister-in-law helped *her* sister-in-law deliver a baby boy born without a brain, his face collapsed almost into his neck. She watched her nephew fight for a life that could not be, just like she watched her babies.

I don't forget all of this in my disappointment. I couldn't. I see it when I close my eyes, because I know this is a baby and it doesn't matter boy or girl. It matters healthy and strong and alive.

We are a few months from welcoming the next boy to our pack, and still the disappointment lingers at the edges. Maybe it always will. But excitement has begun peering in, like a friend waiting to be welcomed, because we know the truth of this boy.

We know he was given by a God who sees the end instead of just the beginning. He was given by a God who believes another Toalson boy is what the world needs. He was given by a God who stretches a mama heart wide and long and deep so it can enfold all those little boys destroying her home. Destroying her life.

These little boys, these amazing little humans I get to call my sons, are the ones who rearrange my world in the exact ways I need. They are the ones who strip me of control and throw around chaos like it's their favorite plaything (it probably is) and turn a whole life inside out. They are the ones who are tearing me into pieces and putting me back together right and whole and more beautiful than I was before.

They teach me how to be a woman. How to be a mother. How to be me.

Now one more will join their ranks. One more will love like a hurricane, uprooting and stripping clean and remaking. One more will turn me toward who I was always meant to be.

This baby, this one who was not what we expected, will join his brothers in a wild, courageous, strong tribe of boys, and he will be wanted. Welcomed. Needed. And so very loved.

We wait eagerly for him, this number six, this number last, this boy named Asher Ruben.

On Being an Invisible Mother

So much of what I do, as a mother, goes unseen. I plan our healthy meals and read the labels of everything I put in my shopping cart, to make sure our home stays toxin-free, and I mix our own cleaners and make note of when we'll need to reorder those essential oils we use for healing. I carve out a schedule that protects our family playing time, and I craft a budget that means we have food and shelter for another month, and I make sure all the art supplies stay stocked.

I manage Amazon subscriptions for ingredient-approved vitamins and count them out every single day and line them up next to my boys' breakfast plates, and instead of "thank you" I hear about how they didn't want these scrambled eggs this morning because all their friends get to eat cereal for breakfast, and why can't they? I clear out their closets when their old clothes are too small, and I buy them new underwear when the old ones cut off circulation and I stock new socks when the old ones have too many holes, and the only thing I hear for it is how they wanted red socks instead of the black ones I bought.

I turn off lights and flush toilets and mend their blankets and remind them to brush their teeth and find their lost library books and read stories until my throat hurts and send them back to bed a thousand times every single night, and I don't even think they notice.

There are so many days I can feel downright invisible.

Welcome to being a mother.

///

When I was eleven years old, my mom slapped a magnet dry-erase calendar on the front of our white refrigerator.

"Dish schedule," she said.

Our names were written on it in black—Jarrod, Rachel, Ashley, and Mom switching places on all the squares. Every month she sat down with a school calendar and the dry-erase one and wrote our names on the schedule in a way that wouldn't interfere with our lives.

The schedule got more complicated when we got to high school, because there were volleyball games and every-night-of-the-week practices and football games with the marching band and National Honor Society and Wednesday night church and homework after all that.

I didn't appreciate all the hard work that went into a schedule as complicated as that. All I did was resent that I had to wash dishes two nights a week. I resented that I worked so hard at school all day and then slaved away at volleyball practice and rode a bus to the pick-up point and finally got home after dark to finish what homework I couldn't do on the bus, because I cared about handwriting and the bus was too bouncy, and then I still had to do the dishes.

So unfair.

My tunnel vision didn't let me see that she worked all day, much harder than I ever did at school, and then she cooked dinner and tried to keep it warm for me and drove to meet the bus and stayed near while I finished my homework so I'd have help if I needed it and, on top of all that, she planned meals for the month and did all the shopping and budgeted our very limited resources and wrote out a schedule for doing dishes so one person was not overburdened with the responsibility.

She was a mother.

She was invisible, too.

///

Now that I have children of my own, I know just how selfish children can be. I know just how thankless motherhood is. I know how no matter what we do behind the scenes, there is still more they want us to do.

It's simply the nature of children. I know this. They don't see their own selfishness or the way those ill-timed complaints can make a mama not ever want to cook a hot breakfast for them ever again or how the mere thought of tackling eight loads of laundry that come back every week is enough to keep her in bed when the alarm chimes. They only wonder why they're having oatmeal again when today was supposed to be pancake-day. They don't see that Mama ran out of time to flip pancakes because she had to turn every male shirt right-side out before sorting it into laundry piles she'll spend all day washing.

It's completely, developmentally normal for them to not make those connections yet. Someday they will.

But someday means nothing for this day, this day I stripped all his sheets and blankets and spent half the day he was at school vacuuming and washing and putting a bed back together because he woke up with ant bites all over his legs and I'm afraid there might be ants in his bed because they were eating popcorn up here yesterday even though it's against the rules. This day he comes out of his room complaining that his blanket is still a little wet.

This day when I loaded the washer with that first pile holding his Spider-Man shirt, because I was sure he'd want to wear it on his birthday, and there's just enough time to wash and dry it before he has to leave for school. This day he comes down the stairs crying about how he can't find his workout clothes to wear on his birthday, and I know they're lying at the bottom of another pile I planned to wash later today.

This day I woke up to find three lights left on all night and I can't help but mentally calculate how much that's going to cost me.

The promise of someday does not make this day any easier.

///

We Count it All Joy

After I married and had an apartment of my own, my mom came visiting with a box.

"What's that?" I said, because I had recently finished unpacking, and I hadn't missed anything important.

"All your old stories," she said.

"What stories?" I said.

"The ones you wrote when you were little," she said, and she pulled out one that imagined what I would do if I had a million dollars. I'd written it when I was seven.

"I'd buy a car, and I wouldn't share with my brother," I'd written. We laughed about it.

There were *Little House on the Prairie* imitations and the story about a girl miraculously walking again to save her friends from danger and another scrawled out on notebook paper the summer I went to visit my dad.

"I didn't know you kept all these," I said.

My mom smiled. "Of course I did."

Of course she did. They were pieces of me she loved. They were pieces that proved her love.

And she is a mother.

///

There is a drawer in my closet where I keep my kids' drawings and old writing notebooks they've filled with words and loose papers with quirky doodles filling corners. My boys don't know the drawer is there.

My eight-year-old doesn't know that when he slipped his note under our bedroom door, the one that bears a picture of a boy with a red face and smoke coming out of his ears and the words, "I feel angry when you tell me it's bedtime," the note went into that drawer. My six-year-old doesn't know that when he wrote a kindergarten essay in school about how he knows his mom loves him when she reads to him, his essay went into that drawer. My four-year-old doesn't know that when the amazing fox picture he drew disappeared from his drawing binder it went into that drawer.

They don't know all the ways I love them, because they are still young children who believe love looks mostly like hugs and kisses and sweet snuggles. They don't know yet that it actually looks like time and service and invisibility.

What I am still learning in my mother journey is that sometimes the greatest acts of love are the ones that whisper instead of shout.

A storage container with writing treasures shoved under our mom's bed.

A dish schedule that honored our time over her own.

A ride to early-morning volleyball practices, even though she worked late.

I want to be that kind of great.

Indignation comes welling up in me, every now and then, when I'm tired and frustrated and annoyed that I can't seem to find a single minute to myself. I want to be noticed. Acknowledged. Appreciated. I forget that invisibility is better than alone.

I get to be a mama. I get to love my children through olive oil brushed over broccoli and a sprinkling of sea salt sitting on top. I get to love them by joining them at the table and coloring a picture of Lightning McQueen, even though a thousand other responsibilities are calling my name. I get to love them with a secret drawer that holds treasures more valuable than what sits in our bank account.

I get to be loved by his bursting into the room while I'm working so he can give me a missed-you kiss. I get to be loved by the flower he brings me, because its beauty reminded him of me, and I get to watch it curl up while I'm writing. I get to be loved in his request to be carried downstairs, just like old times, even though he's so much heavier now and, also, fully capable of walking himself.

I get to be loved in a million silent ways, and I get to love in a million silent ways.

Welcome to being a mother.

On the Second Son

Today he turns six, this second boy who stole my heart.

It's hard to believe he is so old. Every time I look at him now I see a boy, not even little anymore. Just a boy with skinny little legs and big feet and a smile that can light the whole house on fire. Time has flown so fast I want to grab it all back. I want to savor it right now, this moment. I want to hold him while he will still let me, but the problem is, I won't ever want to let him go.

This weekend we cut a cookie cake and played Spider-Man games and watched him open presents like LEGO Spider-Man sets instead of baby blocks, and I kept thinking about how these last six years have gone and how the next six will go, and I feel sad and glad and scared and excited all at the same time.

He is one of the most remarkable children I have ever known.

Just the other day, when I was in the middle of beating myself up about a to-do list largely left undone, with the potential to derail a whole week's plans, in walked my boy, just home from school, with a yellow flower he'd made and another he'd picked. He was grinning.

"I know you're working," he said. "But this is for you."

He kissed me and wrapped his arms around me in a tight hug, and then he was gone.

For six years I have watched this boy grow into his name. *Asa. Healer.*

For six years he has been healing holes in our home.

///

We didn't even know if it was the right time to try for another baby. Four months before, I had lost my grandmother, and I was still reeling from her death, weeping every time someone mentioned the name "Grandma," even though she was called Memaw.

And, at the heart of that yes-we-should-have-another-baby-or-no-we-shouldn't, I was afraid I could not love another child as deeply as I loved the first. Most mothers of one child worry about this, because, until it happens, we cannot imagine how a heart can expand its body borders so it's wide enough to hold multiple children.

But then I took a pregnancy test, and it said no, and I cried, afraid we wouldn't be able to have another baby because so many friends couldn't. That's when I knew just how much I wanted another.

Two weeks later I took another pregnancy test, convinced the first one was wrong because I could hardly climb out of bed in the morning and I fell asleep while my eighteen-month-old was eating his lunch even though my fear of a child choking is right up there with a drowning fear and a getting-hit-by-a-car fear. This time the test said yes and I smiled a little, knowing already who he would be.

He would be called Asa. *Healer.* Zane. *Everything that is good and beautiful.*

Already, just a few weeks in, this baby was healing my heart, glowing new life in the space my Memaw had taken with her. I knew she would want me to be happy, even in grief. And so I let myself be, waiting to meet another little piece of perfection that might carry her generosity or her sharp eyes or that infectious laugh.

///

He doesn't even know all the ways he has healed.

In our home, this second boy is the one who walks in from school and tells each one of his younger brothers how much he missed them while he was away. He is the one who will catch me unaware when I am lost in thought, washing the dishes that never seem to ever be done, and tell me, "You're doing such a great job washing those dishes, Mama" and make me actually want to do them. He is the one who will open doors for his brothers and turn on light switches for the ones too short to reach them and comfort the baby when he's crying.

He has more friends than I can keep up with, and he's the example his teacher uses for a helpful spirit and a kind heart, and he's more often than not an objective mediator between his fist-fighting siblings.

When I asked him today what he's been put on this earth to do, his answer was simple and lovely, an honest picture of who he is at heart.

"To help people," he said.

Yes. Of course. He has been living into that purpose since he was born.

///

He slid into the world after six hours of labor and three good pushes. He was the easiest labor of all.

When they put him in my arms, though, I thought they'd made a mistake. *This isn't my baby,* I thought. *He doesn't look anything like the other one.*

My bond with my first son was instantaneous and deep, and I realized later it was because looking at him was like looking into a time-machine mirror of me as a baby. But this second one had blue eyes that would stay blue and the full lips of his daddy and no hair at all and red splotches all over his body from a labor quick and jarring. I worried that I would not be able to love him after all.

But I shouldn't have worried. My love bloomed and uncurled over those days and weeks and months that followed his birthing day. It was easy to love him. He smiled before any of the others, and he let me hold him as much as I wanted, and there was something in those eyes that could give such courage to an overwhelmed-mama heart.

When his older brother threw a fit because he was tired of sharing Mama's attention, my baby waited calmly to be fed, like it was no big deal. When my belly started growing with baby number three a mere five months after he was born, he simply watched in awe and, later, excitement that there would be another person in our house. When his mama could not play blocks with him because she had to feed the new baby, even though *he* was still a baby, he did not fuss or throw blocks in anger like his older brother would have done in his place. Instead, he came to sit by me, kissing his brother's forehead and waiting for the time when Mama would be free to play.

He is the easiest boy I've ever had.

///

There is a danger in this easy. Sometimes we forget that he has needs, too, because he is kind and calm and flexible and unworried and sweet, a personality that often gets lost in all our crazy. Sometimes we forget that he has his own plans, because he is so good at following everyone else's. Sometimes we forget that he should not always be expected to act like who he is.

We've tried to remind him of this every now and then, because the danger in going with the flow and doing what you're told all the time and always behaving in the way that's expected is that you never get to try out rebellion. Rebellion can be good for us, when used well. It can teach us that we are loved not for our abilities and our behaviors but for simply being us. It can teach us that we are accepted for who we are and not who others expect us to be. It can teach us that we have room to make mistakes, too.

Encouraging rebellion in this precious boy has taken intention and hard work, because he's the kid who's happy to stand in front of his whole school and accept a Star award for exemplary behavior and obedience. But this year I have watched him grow from a boy who had to make sure he was doing everything perfectly right before he tried anything new to a boy who, if not gladly, then at least willingly, leaps into the unknown. I have watched him decide for himself that his art is good—phenomenal, even. I have watched him test limits and slide into a new understanding of what it means to grow up and make his own decisions.

How beautiful it's been.

And through it all he has remained a healer. Everything that is good and beautiful.

On Love that is No Fairy Tale

It's the familiar smell of his skin, the way it stretches across his back, just waiting for my touch; and it's his arms wrapping all the way around me, even when I've been a little crazy and weepy and anxious; and it's his voice, filling the house with music always. It's the way he keeps hope when I can't seem to find mine, the way he believes in the me I was created to be when I'm acting like a not-so-nice piece of the whole, the way he trusts me with something as fragile as his heart.

He's there beside me, watching "The Walking Dead" when I go to sleep in the evening, and he's there, breathing his own dreams, when I open my eyes.

This man with curly black hair and six days' chin-and-cheek stubble and pure-and-devoted love is mine, a gift of the greatest significance.

I call him husband. Lover. Friend.

///

Eleven years ago we stood in an old historical church, beneath the warm glow of lamps that turned eyes to diamonds, and we said those vows we wrote each other, and we meant them with every in-love breath we took before speaking. And then we kissed and danced and he ate and I talked, and the time came to drive to the hotel where we shook our way into the married life.

Dawn broke and he could not find the wallet he needed to board the plane for our honeymoon trip, and a groomsman waited for a ride to the airport with us, the newlywed. This wasn't at all what I'd expected twelve hours married.

It was the first time I realized that marriage did not start on a mountaintop like I'd thought. It started at the bottom of a peak, and it was an uphill climb to make those two lives full of twenty-one years of beliefs and ways of living and separate ideas fit cleanly together.

It was going to take some work.

///

There are days we love well, and there are days we don't.

Even after eleven years, we are still learning hidden parts of each other we didn't know before, like how sometimes all he needs is one encouraging word to believe he can conquer the whole world in a day, like how his heart does not beat so much as sing for all the music bound up in every inch of his body, like how he prefers his frozen yogurt with hot fudge and peanut butter cups and Butterfinger crumbs and Reese's pieces poured liberally on top.

Like how he can capture the attention of our sons for hours at a time with old when-Daddy-was-a-little-boy stories and how sometimes he puts plates with food scraps in the sink side instead of the disposal side and how he tries hard to hide his anxiety but it's still there, even though he never showed he worried at all.

There are days we are each other's best friends, but there are also days we are each other's worst enemies.

And maybe we don't always like each other (because what friends always do?) and maybe sometimes what we do annoys the other, and maybe sometimes we wonder what we could possibly have been thinking all those years ago, but there is something that threads through all those bad days and good days alike.

It is love and forgiveness and belonging.

It is forever.

No matter how many days we have logged forgetting what we knew surely eleven years ago, no matter how many weeks scream exactly the opposite, no matter how many months we ask the hard questions in the hidden parts of our minds, there is a truth we know: we were made for each other.

His positivity made for my negativity. His acceptance made for my perfectionism. His dreaming made for my realism.

His eyes made for my body. My words made for his heart. His soul made for mine.

Even on the worst of days, this truth lights the dark.

///

We Count it All Joy

It didn't take us long to find our first fight.

He worked as a youth and music minister at a church on weekends and a personal banker on weekdays while I spent my days writing stories at the city's largest newspaper. There came a day when we planned to take care of some errands, because the church had handed him his monthly check that morning and we needed to deposit it so we could pay rent.

Except when he opened the planner where he thought he'd put it, the check wasn't there.

Rent was due in two days, and, without that check, we didn't have the money in our account to pay it. And my mind ran fast and furious from no money to no home to trying to keep a marriage together on the streets. I sprawled on our marriage bed like the whole world was ending and he searched the entire house and still didn't find it. He didn't know all the words that swam through my head that day.

He can't keep track of a check.
He can't take care of us.
How will I live with this?

For richer or poorer: is this what those vows meant? I didn't know if I could do it.

///

Those thoughts can feel like a fire, burning love on its altar, because there are expectations we hold like they are life and death.

Of course this shared life will never be perfectly wonderful, because we are two different people with two different backgrounds and two different personalities, and who can ever be fully themselves all the time, every day? We all struggle to remember who we are.

Of course our partner will not be able to measure up to who we thought they'd be the day of our wedding. Neither do we measure up to the person they thought we'd be. Wedding days are for idealistic dreaming, and the rest of the marriage is for realistic loving.

Of course there are days we'll think it's easier to throw in the towel, because we are human and we don't always love like we should. Marriage isn't always easy.

If all we ever do is see the ways he does not measure up to our expectations, how this marriage does not measure up to our idea of happy, how these days spent together are not anything like we'd imagined them to be, we will never make our marriage work. Maybe it will take a year or five or fifteen, but that crumbling will catch up, and we will be burned in the fire of discontent.

The truth of marriage is that not every day is beautiful and smooth and light-filled. Some days are ugly and thorny and chock full of a darkness where thoughts and attitudes and beliefs will trip us up, and we will wonder if this one is really The One.

But there is a part of love that doesn't make the least bit of sense, and sometimes we simply have to keep climbing, arm locked in arm, up that so-hard hill to forever, because the top of the world is still waiting, and it is still for us. We can't look down or back. We only look at each other, and when we see those eyes that still, even today, shine like diamonds, we know.

This is pressing on toward real love.

///

One day he and all the other guys in our folk-rock band quit their full-time jobs, because we were going to travel, we were going to see the world, we were going to share our music with all who would listen.

Except, for us, there was a baby already and another on the way.

So I held on to my steady income. We needed something, some way to pay bills, and my job was flexible and allowed travel, so it made sense that I'd be the one to work along with the play.

Year after year after year I spent working a job and caring for a baby and then two and three and five, traveling to play music in all the margins, and my dream to write sat stiffening under the weight of impossibility. There was no time to pursue my dream, because we were pursuing his, and someone needed to collect a steady income.

And then one day I sat exploding in a prayer session, because my dream had remained stagnant, buckling under the weight of longing for much too long, and I felt the cold bitterness that came with knowing it might not ever be my time. The strength of my resentment surprised me.

If this was for better or for worse, what would I choose from here?

///

It was a whole week of arguing, what felt like one big fight that was really lots of little ones. There were plenty of reasons for it. We were drowning under the overwhelm of brand new twins added to three other little ones. We walked through the house out of sync and exhausted and wound up too tight. And then came the night it was all too much, and I slammed the bedroom door and he walked out the front and I heard the car rev and those tires squeal, and I thought it was the last we'd see of him.

It was a night just like that when it was the last we saw of my dad.

We both come from a long line of divorce, generations of people giving up on each other, people walking out on each other, people choosing others over their beloved. What makes us any different?

The end dates of marriages visit me in subtle ways I can hardly name, like shadows I can't shake, fourteen years for my parents, fewer for his.

What makes us any different?

I cried into my pillow that too-much-fighting night, and it felt like hours but was really only minutes before he came back and wrapped me in his warmth and said the words it always comes back to. *I love you.*

I sat up in our bed and faced him and my fears. I told him what I think about when those years of our parents come and go. He looked at me and pressed my hand and said, *We are not them. Their story is not our story.*

We come from these backgrounds, and we carry around these cracked hearts, and we feel those pasts like they somehow tell our futures, but the truth is we make our own stories. We are not what has come before. We are not even what comes after, at least not right now. We are who we are in this moment right here, this moment where we choose love and forgiveness and reconciliation or we choose to turn our backs and let marriage fold in on itself.

We are our own story, and just because my parents only made it fourteen years doesn't mean our love has the same expiration date or that it holds an ending at all. Our love story is full of its own twists and turns and whole years of unexpected, but it is ours to make and choose.

So today, five days from marking eleven years of love, I remember that I would choose it all over again, this love that is hard and wild and strong and brave, this love that burns away all the pieces of two lives that don't belong to the shared one, this love that walks us steady toward the top of forever.

I choose him still. Now. Always.

On Being a Mother of Only Boys

It happens unexpectedly, like everything else this boy does.

The oldest, the one who first stole my heart, sits on the side of my bed during our snuggle time. He is drawing some cartoons for the book we're brainstorming, one we plan to write together. He says it almost like it's an afterthought, like it isn't a big deal, because he has no way of knowing how big it is.

"I want to marry a woman like you when I grow up," he says. I laugh and touch his cheek, and he smiles wide into my eyes. "Really," he says. "I'm not joking."

I know he's not, so I tell him so. And then, when the timer clangs and the baby starts fussing to be fed and he walks out, back to his room, I breathe deep and long, trying to keep the tears from dropping. They do anyway.

Maybe it's because the last few days he's been walking around the house reminding us he only has eight more years before he's driving and ten more years before he graduates. I'm not ready for any of it. I'm not ready for them to be grown. I'm not ready for them to be married. I'm not ready for them to be gone.

Sure, he's only eight, but the day is speeding upon us, if

the last eight years have anything at all to teach us. One day he will be gone. One day they will all be gone. They will all be someone else's.

This is all right and true and noble and sweet and beautiful. But there is a bittersweet piece to it.

They are all boys. So I will lose them all.

///

When I was a senior in college, I came down with a severe case of the flu. I had never before had the flu, in all my twenty-one years. My throat felt scaly and fire-filled, my cheeks turned red, and I could not sleep my body hurt so badly. My husband, who was just a fiancé at the time, stuck by my side, even at the risk of getting sick himself. He put a cold washcloth on my head, to keep the fever down. He made me hot soup and fed me the two bites I could swallow. He took me to the emergency room when my fever got so high I almost passed out. And then, when it got too much to bear, I finally croaked out, "Call my mom."

There is something about your mom knowing you're sick that makes you feel the tiniest bit better. She doesn't even have to drive the one hundred twenty-three miles to your college apartment or sit on the side of your bed or wait outside the room while you sleep. She just has to know.

A few weeks later, my husband, who was still only a fiancé at the time, came down with a stomach virus and puked for days. The only person he called was me. His mother didn't even know.

///

I ask my friends with grown boys all the time.

Does he call?

Does he visit?

Does he invite you to visit?

Do you know when he's sick?

Do you know when he's hurt?

Do you see him at all?

Most of their answers are the same. *Not often,* they say.

I don't know if it will be the same with my boys. But I do know that the bond between a mother and a daughter in those growing up years grows right up with them. The daughters have children, and we begin to understand what our mother sacrificed and how deeply she loved and how hard it all was.

My boys will never know what it's like to be a mother, only what it's like to be a father. They will never feel what I felt, that incredible awe at having grown this perfect little human being and how lovely it was to watch them eat in the lamplight of my room and the way they grew me into a better version of myself.

I used to think I was missing something, that this piece of motherhood—becoming the mother of a daughter—had been withheld because I was not good enough to raise a girl. Now I know better.

Every child is a great gift, and whether or not we receive him as such doesn't change the truth of that gift. They were all given so they could scrape us into the best versions of ourselves, and maybe they are boys and maybe they are girls, but they all scrape our hearts the same.

If my boys want to marry a woman like me someday, then I have to let them shape who I become.

///

When my first pregnancy test showed positive, and my husband and I could finally move again, my mother was the first person we called. He was the first grandchild, so of course she was excited. She went to the second appointment with me and listened to his heartbeat. We recorded the first sonogram and gave her a copy. She called me every week, and I called her in between to let her know how I was doing.

She was the one I wanted to stay with me after the baby came home so we could find our feet with this new little person. She was the one who comforted me when my milk never came in. She was the only one I trusted to keep him for the first overnight road trip his daddy and I took.

Having a baby made our bond even stronger, and I ached to have a little girl so I could one day share that with her, too. So I could tell her about the incredibly strong women whose genes she shared.

Only it didn't happen.

We welcomed boy after boy after boy, and the one girl

who came slipped right through our hearts before we could meet her. And then came more boys.

Mother of a daughter is a title I would not carry.

///

This is our last baby. I knew it was coming, and even though I felt disappointed at first that the baby I carried was a boy, I am *so very glad* that he is another boy.

But.

There is still a deep longing for the daughter I lost, for the bond I missed, for a lifelong friendship like the one I share with my mother. People often ask, when they see or hear that we are the parents of six boys: "Did you want a girl?"

The answer is of course. Of course I wanted a daughter. Of course I wanted to raise a girl to know where she stands in a world that was made for men. Of course I wanted to raise a girl to know she didn't have to do anything at all to be proved worthy. Of course I wanted to raise a girl so she would know she was beautiful even in all the imperfect places. It's not the reason we had six children, but I did want to be the mother of a daughter.

A daughter shares something so very special with her mother, and I wanted this. She shares the experience of seeing her mother sitting in the stands at all her basketball games, even the ones where she sat the bench for too many aggressive fouls. She shares the experience of accepting a "secret" engagement and understanding, later, that her mother knew all along, because a mother always knows.

She shares the experience of having watched her mother put food on the table, day after day, week after week, year after year, and, once she has children, knowing a little something about this overwhelming need to provide them with everything they need.

I will never have a daughter to experience a first heartbreak with, and I will never have a daughter whose engagement I know about first, and I will never have a daughter bounce career ideas off me.

I will not be the one they call when they are sick. I will not be the one they open up to about the girl they think they might love. I will not be the first one to know they are getting married or having a baby or what gender the baby will be or what they're doing for Christmas or how long he's had the flu.

It's okay to grieve this, because it is a hard knowing. And it's only in admitting what we want and how we didn't quite get it exactly that we can clear our eyes enough to see that what we want and what we need are two very different things.

So I am a mother of only boys.

This is something wonderful, too.

///

One day my boys may marry a woman like me. And I will be right there, cheering from the sidelines, next to their daddy, waiting for them to call me or visit me or share with me—or not.

Whatever that future holds doesn't change the truth of now: I have been given a great gift, because I am a mother. I don't have to live in those future days now. I don't have to pretend I know how they will end up. I don't have to look at my boys now and see them all grown up, pulling away, because the truth is, I have no idea what my sons all grown up will look like.

I only know that right now they are my boys. They are my boys *right now*.

One day they will be gone, but that isn't today. So today I will enjoy being the mama of these boys I love so much my heart feels too big for my chest. I will enjoy being the first one they run to when they're hurt and the first one they tell when they have some exciting news and the only one they want to hold them when they're sick.

Yes. This is something wonderful, too.

On Parenting a Spirited Child

We walk into the school, turning the corner down toward his classroom, and I can feel the tension and sadness pulsing through his hand in mine. When I turn to him for this morning goodbye, his pupils are so large his eyes look nearly black.

By this time next week, my boy will be in a new classroom, with a new teacher, with new anxieties sitting on his chest.

Today, he will walk into his old classroom, after three days in school suspension for a mistake he made that was sorely misinterpreted, and he will sit at his old desk and he will look around at those old classmates he's shared a room with for two years, and he will know that it is his last day here, with a teacher he loved but who no longer has the patience and stamina to handle his emotional outbursts.

This morning I can't even make it all the way to his door because of the emotions clogging my throat, pulling tears from their unending reservoir down my cheeks, so I stop, two rooms away. The only person I see in this crowded hallway is my son, trying to breathe, trying to be brave, trying to overcome all this rejection and misunderstanding and a label that, already, sticks hard to his seven-year-old back.

I try not to let him see my tears, brushing them away quickly like I did this morning, when he showed me the note he'd written to his teacher—a picture of her in a classroom and him sitting at a desk, crying, and a thick wall between them, underlined by a few words: *I will miss you.*

But he feels their water trail when I bend over him and press my face to his and whisper the same words I've whispered in his ear every morning before dropping him off: *Remember who you are. Strong. Kind. Courageous. And most of all my son.*

And then I watch him walk through that classroom door for the last time, not sure how this day will go after the last sixteen.

Will he remember who he is, or will he remember who they say he is?

They are two very different things.

///

Four days ago I sat in an office with the school principal and her assistant principal to talk about the latest of my son's conduct violations, misinterpreted from my perspective. But it joins fifteen other conduct violations—for tearing up his already-graded homework when he felt angry, signing his name as "stupid jerk" when he felt sad, and collapsing into a crying pile on the floor when he didn't get to use the magnifying glass for his science project like everyone else in the class did—in the last twenty days.

They are telling me something must be done because his classmates are afraid of him and his teacher doesn't think she's a good fit for him anymore and all of it is against the school's code of conduct.

This boy has always been our spirited child, and his daddy and I have worked diligently over the years to give him the tools and space and practice to handle his big emotions, but there are days and whole weeks sometimes when those big emotions grip him and refuse to let go.

I try to tell them what we've learned from each of the write-up incidents, at least the four of them we've seen. The story, from his perspective, tells much more than those words written on a discipline violation page, but how do you argue with a school administration that sees only the bad behavior and not the boy behind them?

This last incident, the worst of them, happened when it was leaving time. He was finishing up an art project, his favorite kind of project, trying to cut out his picture before he needed to pack up. The substitute teacher, probably frustrated by his lack of obedience, tried to grab the scissors away from him, but he beat her to it, throwing them into a corner of the room. Fortunately, no classmates happened to be in this corner because they were all packing up their backpacks like they were supposed to be doing, a disaster averted. But then he ran out of the room to escape the fire of his own anger.

The sub, who had been "warned confidentially" about

him, did not talk to my son about his outburst but, instead, wrote up a conduct report of her own observations and assumptions. She never considered why he might have felt the way he did or why he chose to express himself that way or what emotion might have caused a little boy to run away.

And it's not okay—of course it's not. Children shouldn't throw scissors, even if they're blunt-tipped, anywhere near other children. Children shouldn't run from a room where a teacher is charged with keeping students safe. But kids, I believe (and psychology has begun to prove), always have a reason for what they do, and the reason is often buried so far down it has to be dragged out with skillful fingers.

Sometimes the meltdown can be prevented in the first place by a word or two about how hard it is to put down an art project when there are no minutes left for working, instead of grabbing scissors from the hands of a focused boy. It's always worth a try.

The administrators, in the meeting, said they wanted him to stay in school suspension for three days for this latest incident, so he'll "learn his lesson this time." And I can't help but wonder what this lesson is that we're trying to teach. He is seven years old. At the depths of his heart, he doesn't want to mishandle his emotions or scare people or spend a whole day or three of them in isolation from all the people he loves.

He slumped against me when I broke the news that he

would not be returning to class just yet. He didn't understand. I tried to help him understand.

"Your substitute teacher thought you were threatening her," I explained.

"But I wasn't," he said, his eyes filling with tears.

"I think she might have misinterpreted what you were trying to do," I said.

"She thinks I'm bad," he said, and then I was blinking tears away.

I read the despair in his eyes that day, and I could physically feel the giving up, the hopelessness waiting around the corner. How does a kid who's led to believe he's the "bad kid" ever become anything but a bad kid?

The question stood between me and school administrators that day.

So I pulled him tight against me, and I held him through the words he sobbed: *I just don't understand why they don't believe me. I didn't do what the substitute says I did.* And then I held him through all the minutes after, when big emotions shook his body quiet.

I told him that sometimes what we intend to say with our words and actions and what others interpret are two very different things, and we have to be careful about how we come across. I don't even know if he understands this communication nuance, because he's seven years old. And then the bell rang and it was time to leave, and his little brothers were still waiting patiently for the walk home.

But before I left, I whispered words I hoped would stay with him all day in the quiet of an isolation room: *You are loved deeply. Remember who you are. You are not these mistakes, ever.*

It hurt my heart to leave him in that room all by himself, but I did.

I cried all the way home.

///

Once upon a time, when I was a senior in college, I substituted for a "troubled" school district near my university. Every time I took a job, there were students the teacher warned me about. And all day long I would wait for the trouble.

It would always come.

I was quick to write up those conduct violation sheets, because I had been warned it would probably happen, and I'd been shown where they were kept, and I'd been directed how exactly to fill them out.

I know now that those problems probably came because the kids knew I was watching, since someone was always watching. They knew I was waiting, because someone was always waiting. They knew that whatever they did they wouldn't be able to win—my word against theirs, no matter their intent.

When you believe a kid is a problem, all you'll ever see is the problem.

I wish I could go back to all those kids I sent to the office with a condemnation sheet in their hands. I wish I could tell them, *You are more than this problem they warned me about. I believe you can do better. And I am not waiting for you to fail. I am waiting for an opportunity to help you succeed.*

I feel sad that my young son is that kid, but being on this side of it helps me to see that they weren't just "problem kids" like we teachers were trained to believe. They are not problems to be solved. They are little precious people crying out for help because of emotions and circumstances too big for them to understand and talk about.

That doesn't mean that what they do to communicate their plea for help is right. But it does mean that we, the adults, have a responsibility: to become a child and see from their perspective and always assume good intent, because sometimes what we see a child doing and what they think they're doing are not the same thing.

I wish I had known this back then. I wonder how it might have changed the lives of those "problem" kids.

///

My boy has been through a lot in his short seven-year life.

There was a sister-death when he was four. There was a twin pregnancy, a few months later, when a mama was in and out of hospitals and doctors' offices because we thought we'd lost them and we hadn't and we thought we'd lost them again and we hadn't, and then they were finally here, and they spent twenty days in the neonatal intensive care unit, and a mama and daddy left boys with a rotating babysitter every night so we could spend two hours with the tiny babies who needed us in that short window of time. And then those twins came home, and I don't think any of us even remember the whole first year of the twins' life, because everything blurred into chaotic oblivion.

In the middle of that chaotic year he started school. It was a brand new environment not so different from home in terms of noise and bodies, but also widely different because there were twenty-four other students a boy could get lost behind. My best guess is it was overwhelming, overstimulating, and, perhaps, somewhat unbearable for a boy who valued working on his own in a quiet space.

His actions said what he could not say: *Help me. Help me process what I'm feeling. Help me feel understood. Help me know what to do with these overwhelming emotions.* And no one in those classes would listen, because they were there to learn, not to heal, and a boy, five years old, built up his armor so efficiently nothing could penetrate it.

Which brings us here, to a place where a boy's armor is starting to crack. This boy doesn't know how to deal with those pieces he's hidden for so long, pieces that are leaking out faster than he can patch the hole.

This is the reality that isn't shown on a conduct violation sheet.

When I started my parenting journey, I never thought I would be the parent of a child who had trouble in school, a child who is brilliant beyond his age and gets all the right grades, a child who is a minefield of emotions.

I probably should have.

I was a kid who preferred a room of five or six to a room of twenty-four. I was a teenager who preferred staying home to read *Wuthering Heights* and *Pride and Prejudice* and *Doctor Zhivago* out back in the hammock, rather than going out with friends. I am still the woman who waits in the school pickup line with my heart pounding, hoping no one will look me in the eye, because then I might have to talk, and I hate small talk.

I often wonder how I, a big emotion, highly sensitive introvert, would have fared in today's classroom of pods and constant group activities and no real space of my own. It's no wonder my boy, walking around with a fever of frustration, wondering where he really belongs, over-stimulated on an hourly basis, is crying so loudly for help.

And when a child cries for help, we must listen first and "fix" later.

Sometimes there are ways to bully a boy that have nothing to do with fists and words and threats that scare him into cooperation. Sometimes there are lonely lunch tables and sitting out the fifteen minutes of recess he needs and isolating him in an office for three days. Sometimes bullying can look like kids tattling five times a day on the one boy they've learned will always get in trouble, the one teachers will always believe did something wrong.

Sometimes bullying can look like writing up a boy sixteen times in twenty days without asking the question, "Why is this happening?"

No kid is born a bad kid.

And if all we're doing is writing up a kid for a behavior violation, and we're not doing the work to find out why that behavior violation might have happened, we all lose.

///

Last night my boy sat in his bed while his daddy and I tucked him in. It was there we told him he'd be changing classrooms. His first words were, *What if I'm sent to the office again?*

And then he cried and begged not to go to school anymore. He is seven years old, for God's sake.

He is seven years old, and in his mind, everything he does anymore means he'll get told on by another student. Every action he chooses is the wrong one. Everything about him is unacceptable. His eyes tell me this. I can hardly bear it.

How does a parent speak truth into a heart that believes he's a problem, an inconvenience, a "bad kid" who will never learn to control his impulses because this is what all those discipline write-ups in a twenty-day history tell him, and this is what a teacher not wanting him anymore tells him, and this is what an in-school suspension sentence tells him.

How do you convince a child that he is loved, that he is

good, that he is more than his seven-year-old mistakes, when those conduct violation sheets tell him a different story?

The question follows me into sleep.

And there is a dream, like there has often been on nights I needed to know something—when I saw my brother's overturned vehicle in a dream before his car accident, when I dreamed of waves too high and dangerous and begged him not to go on his deep-sea fishing trip, when I saw my third son lying in a baby swing with his head wrapped in a bandage weeks before that head injury happened in a church nursery.

This one is no less clear.

In it, we were walking down his school hallway, and in the flash of a moment, I had his new baby brother, Asher, in my arms. He was minutes old. I sat down with my oldest boy at the door of his classroom, and he was very gentle and sweet. He leaned down to kiss Asher and said his brother's name once.

Then he sat back against the brick wall, and his face got red, and his eyes filled with pain and tears, and he said his newest brother's name again. "Asher," he said, except this time his voice filled with sadness and despair. I knew what to do in my dream. I put Asher down in the middle of the hallway, and I took my biggest one in my arms instead. I held him for as long as he sobbed, which was a long, long time.

I woke to an answer that felt clear and awful, all at the same time.

My son has lost his significance in his family at home and his "family" at school, and he is asking for help the only way he knows how. The last three years of his life he has only ever known one brother after another encroaching on his world, and now there will be another. Who is he in the six of them? Who is he in the twenty-four others at school? When will someone listen to hear him? When will someone care enough about his emotional state to help?

Behind all those discipline write-ups, beneath all those words scrawled on a behavior violation page, this is the story told. This is the armor that has begun to crack, because a seven-year-old can only self-repair for so long.

So we are peeling the rest of that armor away. We are rolling away the stone from this grave that sits in the corner of a little boy's heart. We are fighting, in all the ways we can, for a child who is significant and beautiful and precious, no matter the mistakes he has made in the last thirty days.

We are unwrapping the grave clothes. We are whispering truth. We are writing his name on the tablet of his heart: Gift.

Because this is who he is, even if a school system has flagged him as something else entirely. Still we hold him as a gift.

And there is Another who holds him and fights for

him, too. There is Another who will speak his true name and burn up that false one stamped on his back by a world that doesn't understand. There is Another who promised victory.

And so we wait and hope and love in all the spaces we can.

On Miscarriage

It's been more than three years, but there are still flashes that remind me of that day—a song or a word or the way the light falls in a room just so. Tonight it's words that send me back to a bright-white room where a baby, my baby, died.

"You give and take away": these are words that hold sorrow in their hands.

I know what it's like to be given a treasure. I know what it's like to have that treasure taken away. I know what it's like to die in the places no one can see. I know what it's like to stand at the end and wish it was The End.

And it doesn't matter if she was twelve weeks in a womb or twelve years breathing the air of the world, losing a child all hurts the same.

///

It was a Friday. It was a routine doctor's appointment on a sunny summer day. It was the "we made it safely" day according to all the pregnancy books.

There was no blood. There were no cramps. There were no signs that a baby had died wrapped tight in my warmth. There was only a blank screen where a heartbeat had been, where it was supposed to be now, today, because *this was the safe day.*

They sent me home with my horror, and my husband drove me back so they could clean her from the parts of me that had not let her go in the three weeks she'd been dead, and then he wheeled me out of the same place I'd carried out three babies in my arms before this one someone else carried out in a lab jar. This time those hallways turned ugly and the smooth ride hurt and the whole world dimmed.

My husband held me all night, and I woke with a pillow soaked with tears I don't even remember crying, because I thought I was sleeping. All her brothers were knocking on the door because life doesn't care about a whole world ending. It just goes on.

It was a Saturday when my husband called the pastor of the church where we were serving and told him what had happened, that he'd need a Sunday or two off so our family could process through this loss. But there was no bereavement leave for a death like this one. It was just a miscarriage.

It was just a miscarriage, and the unspoken expectation was that he should be able to stand on stage two days after his daughter's death and sing to a God who gives and takes away, like this God hadn't given a daughter and then taken her right back away.

So my husband went. I could not climb from my bed, so I stayed, wrapped up to my chin in a blanket that smelled like him. I cried. I bled. I died a little more in that dark room without him.

Without her.

///

They say we should get over it. They say it's only a miscarriage. They say it should be easier, because at least we didn't carry her for nine months and then watch her die. At least we didn't raise her for nine years and then watch her take that last shudder of a breath. At least we never even had to meet her and look in a face that would be stuck in our memories forever.

Except I do meet her. In dreams. In unguarded moments when I see her squished on the couch between her brothers, reading. In the family picture taken right after our twins, who would have been her little brothers, were born. She is there, with her fiery auburn hair and her summer-evening-sky eyes.

They, the ones who have never been required to make space for this pain in the corner of their hearts, don't understand how a year later I'll be saying her name and I'll get all choked up, still. How two years later I'll hear a song that reminds me of the words I raged from the cold, concrete floor when I actually had strength enough to lift my head and shout, how the hearing-again knocks my legs unsteady. How all these babies, the ones who came before and the ones who have come after, are precious and beautiful and wanted, of course they are, but I still wish I hadn't lost the one.

Losing a baby in the beginning still feels like the end, because it would have been party of six or it would have been three boys and a girl or it would have been a family that looks much different if she were here.

They don't understand that we who have lost babies in utero can't be rushed through this kind of grief, because it is still hard and it is still awful and it is still ugly, ugly, ugly, no matter how many children we have or how much time has passed or how strong we seem to a world that expects only strong. This is a piece of jagged glass we will carry all our days, and we never know when it will pierce us in our tender places again.

We don't need someone to grieve with us. We don't need someone to hurry us. We don't need someone to tell us God will never give us more than we can handle or that all things work together for our good or that He promises us a hope and a future.

We need someone to understand this sorrow, the way it turns a world inside out and pulls out all the seams and unravels everything we've known.

It is a sorrow like any other.

///

There were some who understood.

Four days after that losing day, my husband and I drove out of town for a youth camp. We'd had the worship-leading job booked for a year, and we knew it was too late to find a replacement. So we sent our boys with family and drove all that way in silence, because I could not find the words to speak my sorrow or rage or disappointment or whatever rose to the surface of my roiling heart.

He led worship alone that first night, and I hid in the shadows, watching the moon and letting his words sit on my shoulders. I could not be alone in the dark with all the blood that shouldn't be there. Standing outside, a football field away from students and the man I loved worshiping a God I could not feel in this losing-place, made me feel less alone.

Two women found me huddled beneath a tree. One of them had been through more than just my one loss, and she gripped my hands and prayed over me, there under the boughs of an oak tree that keeps all the secrets of the world. She ended the prayer and then she wrapped me in her arms and whispered some words, and she didn't care that my cheeks were black with the tears that took my makeup all the way down to my chin.

She understood that it would never really go away, the pain. But I would learn to carry on.

///

The minute I took the pregnancy test, I called my husband.

We had decided now was as good a time as any to expand our child count from three to four, and I knew he'd be as excited as I was about what the pregnancy test had to tell us. And he was.

After the first appointment, where her heartbeat showed strong on a screen, we let ourselves settle into the reality of four little ones instead of three. We talked about where she would sit in our car and where she would sleep in our house and what kind of room she would have—a shared one or her own, as the only girl? I picked out the colors I would use to crochet her blanket. I marked the material I'd use for her bibs and dresses and bows.

She was a person, already living in our home.

This is how it happens. We imagine who they will be and how they will fit into our families and whose nose and eyes and hair they will wear. Before we even meet them, we have already planned their details and we have already seen their faces and we have already embraced them, alive.

And then they are gone, and they will never sit in our car or sleep in that bed or look at the walls of the room we decorated with them in mind. There is only a hole where they used to be, and even though our uterus will shrink again and the blood will taper off and our body will forget it ever carried new life within, we will never forget.

We fly right off the edge in the losing, and it takes time to climb back up.

///

We stood in line to check out, one twin seat balanced in the front of the basket, the other inside it, and the woman behind me said, "Such beautiful boys. No girls for you?"

It's an innocent question that typically comes when people see the five boys following me through a store. I turned to answer with my usual, "No. Boys sure are great, though," but my oldest, five years old at the time, beat me to it.

"We have a sister," he said. "She's in heaven with Jesus."

The woman was taken aback by his candor, as we often are with children, and said nothing else. She surreptitiously checked the lines around us, perhaps to see if there was another shorter than ours or perhaps to save face. To her credit, she stayed. And my boy told her how his sister's name is Amarise, which means "given by God," and how she died in Mama's belly and how we never got to meet her but we will someday.

Sometimes it's easier to answer that girl question with a simple no, but I wonder if we are missing a piece of healing here. Her brothers know the truth, that she was and is and will always be their baby sister. She was real. She is real. She is my daughter who died.

Her living was real. Her dying was real. Her memory is real. I hope we never forget.

///

We don't talk about it much, we who have been through the horror of losing a baby we never met, but there are many of us out here, spinning to the floor or trying to lift our heads or finally walking out the other side of that crack in a world.

We don't talk about it because it hurts. We don't talk about it because we're afraid that maybe we did something wrong. We don't talk about it because we should be okay by now, shouldn't we?

I want to tell you that it's okay to feel sad and crushed and sick, sick, sick that your baby is the one who slipped away when there are all those others who aren't wanted or needed or loved. It's okay to grieve.

I want to tell you that you can take as long as you need to get over this loss, even when "they're" telling you you're taking too long and it was only a miscarriage and at least it didn't happen later when it would have been harder to say goodbye.

There is no harder goodbye. There is only hard goodbye.

So grieve. Rage. Cry until your stomach hurts and your eyes feel like they're burning away and you can't even make another sound. Keep that sonogram picture, the one that proves she had a heartbeat once upon a time, the one that says she lived. You'll be glad you did.

It's hard to see from these days and weeks and months after losing that there is another side to this dark, that one day you will mend this crack in your world and you will run your fingers over that scar and feel stronger and more alive because of it.

You will.

But for now, let the world fracture open. Let the light go out. Stay down as long as you need, as long as it takes. Fumble around in the darkness until your eyes adjust and you see the flicker of a candle glowing in a corner, waiting for another day.

And then, only when you feel ready, crawl toward that day, because it is still waiting. Let love walk you back out of the dark.

You learn something important in loss, and it is this: You are so much stronger than you know.

On Childhood Depression

I heard it first in a call from the school psychologist, summoned to get to the bottom of an eight-year-old's acting-out behavior in the classroom two months ago (he was only seven years old when this journey began). But I heard it again in a face-to-face debrief meeting with his current teacher and the school principal and the psychologist, and it's the weight of those ugly words, "I'm not as happy as I used to be" and "Nobody ever listens to me" and "I never seem to do the right thing," collected during an interview between my son and the psychologist, that burn my eyes and the back of my nose.

I try to blink the tears away before all those other calm-and-composed women notice, but I can't do it, because it's my boy, eight years old, and this was not supposed to happen.

Depression was not supposed to happen.

One of the women runs off to get tissues, and I wonder if it's bad enough to make my eco-friendly makeup run, because it's easier to worry about the way a face looks than about the way depression looks.

These hormones, I say, with a little laugh.

And even though I'm eight months pregnant, it's not

the hormones, not really. It's a little boy's words. No mama expects depression in the boy she has loved and adored and cared for and watched and played games with and read to and hugged and kissed, every chance she gets, for eight years and counting.

And yet, it is here.

///

Once upon a time in this mama's child life, there was a boy who exploded with anger, who never wanted anyone to see him cry, even though he was a sensitive boy. This boy worked hard, from a young age, to break free from the grip of darkness.

But there were reasons: there was a dad missing from those most formative years; how does a boy learn to be a man when there is no father to show him? There was a missed-one who called sporadically, making promises that he hardly ever kept; the boy believed them all, because he loved the one who had left, and every time a promise stood broken, the boy crawled deeper into himself, and darkness gained another foothold. There was a mom forced to work multiple jobs just to make ends meet. There were three moves in three years, three starting-overs, three make-new-friends challenges, three learn-how-to-survive-now changes.

One day, when the boy was eleven, he complained of burning pain in his stomach, and his mama took him to the hospital, and doctors found ulcers eating up the belly of a child. His mama called in the troops, a counselor and his teachers at school and the family he loved.

She did her part.

But depression is a tough disease to beat.

///

I know this. I am terrified of it.

I saw the way depression could twist a temper and send it flying out of control. I saw the way it could whisper irrational solutions into the heart of another child. I saw the way it could send a body to bed for days on end. Sometimes forever.

And now, here is my boy, facing this monster.

He comes from a different background than the boy of my youth, but there are still so many pieces in the puzzle of anger turned inward. There is his intelligence, high above his grade level so he feels unchallenged and different and, much of the time, alone. There is his introversion in a house of four, going on five, brothers, where he is hard-pressed to get a word in edgewise, where he can hardly ever find a place of his own. There is his intuition and his sensitivity and his boredom in a traditional classroom and his dreams and his expectations and his behavior and his big emotions and his inability to do anything acceptable, at least from his own perspective. It's no wonder we are here.

It's no wonder he has fallen into this pit.

I am scared to death that he will not be able to find his way back out.

///

One day, that once-upon-a-time boy was riding in the backseat on the way to a counselor's appointment. He was eleven years old, and he already felt crazy, misunderstood, damaged, and this trip proved what he had known all along. There was something wrong with him, something no one could fix.

What if no one could fix it?

He knew the reason he was here: he'd let it slip that he was going to jump off a bridge, and a friend had told. He didn't know if he'd ever feel like not jumping off a bridge.

And maybe he wouldn't have really done it when it came down to it and he peered from the top of a bridge and thought about how much it would hurt to fly, but it didn't matter, at least not that day. Because a mama had seen the look in his eyes, and she recognized it, and she made sure to help him in all the ways she could. Counseling. Time. Love.

///

It was hard to see it, what my son's psychologist found. My boy didn't stay in bed for days on end, and he didn't lose any of his boy-energy. He didn't cry endlessly or isolate himself or lose all interest in life. He just had a short fuse, and he exploded in anger and acted impulsively when anger got the best of him.

There were days when he would open wide and let a mama and daddy see straight to his soul, where he wrestled with thoughts like *No one really likes me* and *I don't belong in this family* and *I should never have been born.* There were days when he sat happily with his brothers playing a game of chess or Battleship or Jenga, and he would crack jokes and smile widely and laugh until his stomach hurt. And then there were other days when he clamped tight, and he sat listening to an audio book for hours on end and immersed himself in creating detailed Twister Man comics and bent over his desk putting together and taking apart and putting together again all those LEGO creations.

It didn't seem all that unusual, but we weren't looking for depression.

This is the kind of thing that can smack a parent in the face and heart and deep, deep down in the gut—because there was another boy who fell into the pit of depression, pushed from behind by a broken family. And we're not a broken family, but we're all broken parents, and what if we caused it? What if our boy never quite recovers because we are still here? What if healing is too far for our love and support and acceptance to reach?

How do I keep him from doing what those others of my past have done?

I don't know. Maybe I never will.

///

No one else was up that night I was reading in the living room and the boy from once upon a time slid past me into the bathroom that could never be locked because the door didn't close all the way.

He was eighteen, I was seventeen. It was another year when a dad had disappeared, just after a call had come telling us he'd been in a work accident, trapped under a tractor that had very nearly crushed him, and then there was nothing, for months on end. We did not know whether he was alive or dead. It was a year when a boy would graduate and life waited and he did not know if he was up to the challenge, even though he was brilliant and talented and could have grabbed any job he wanted. It was a year when a boy would be leaving, growing up, becoming a man, and he wasn't quite sure he knew how.

He was holed up in the bathroom for forty-five minutes or more, and then he walked back out with wraps around his wrists that he tried to hide. I didn't make a sound, but I couldn't breathe from where I sat on the blue-flowered couch. I tried to forget what I had seen, tried to concentrate on the open book in my lap, tried to settle what I knew but didn't want to know.

Still, the tears came hot and thick. I knew what he'd done, what he'd attempted, and hadn't I tried it myself a thousand times, in more subtle ways—starving myself, going whole days and weeks without eating not just because I wanted to be thin but because I wanted them to watch me wasting away? It was the easiest way for me to die.

This was the easiest way for him to die, too.

Something about depression wraps around an ankle and grows like the silence of an evening. It never lets you go.

///

This is not what I want for my son.

Two months ago, at the height of his behavioral issues at school, his daddy and I found a counselor for him. Every week he sits in a room full of toys and he plays and talks and maybe, just a little, heals. And yet today, when I am sitting in that school room, with all those women who don't know him like I do, I listen to them talk about helping him through transitions with a timer and providing him a cool-down place for his big emotions, but all I can hear are those words on repeat in my mind.

My son is depressed. My son is depressed. My son is depressed.

What if?

What if he doesn't beat it?

What if there are darker days ahead?

What if there is suicide?

All these questions can tie a mama in great big, tight knots, but they are the wrong questions for this day, for today. The question today is: What can I do to help my son?

It's a question without a simple answer. Spend more one-on-one time with him. Pursue a hobby together. Understand and accept and fully embrace him, without changing him.

Sometimes part of beating depression away, for a time, is teaching an eight-year-old boy what to do with his anger, how to rise above it, how to feel it and not be afraid of it, how to crawl all the way through it and stand back up on the other side. If all we're told is that our anger is unjustified or wrong or unacceptable, we will do the only thing left. We will turn it inward, and the darkness will get another grip on our heels.

He is a boy with anger huddled somewhere deep inside him, and we must do the work of digging it out, letting it out, dragging out that darkness to the light of day. Every day. Every moment. Every encounter.

We cannot just hope it will change. We cannot pretend it doesn't exist. We cannot hide it. These hearts of our children are worth more than saving face.

And so we sign him up for that extra help at school, and we show up every week to those counseling sessions, and we do everything we can at home to help heal a heart whole.

And there is Another who speaks life into the places where darkness has swallowed the light. There is Another who carries truth into the hearts of men and women and little boys and whole generations. There is Another who lifts their heads and breaks those chains of depression every time they clamp tight. My son knows and loves this Another.

And there will come a day—I know there will—when

my boy will beat this disease. It will not beat him—because he has a future and a hope, and it is good and bright and beautiful.

This is enough for today.

On Raising Twins

I walk into his bedroom, checking on him for the seventh time, interrupting my writing to do it, which means I'm already annoyed. Put out. A touch angry.

Maybe I waited too long to come in here, but there he is, sitting in the middle of a pile of clothes and their hangers. I feel the rage in my shoulders; haven't I told him a thousand times to stay out of closets and drawers and his brothers' beds?

My heart sinks to my toes, and I shake my head. His eyes stare wide, because he knows, *he knows* he's in trouble for this, and then I see the worst of it: a wet spot on the pillow that no longer has a case because he stripped it off before he did his deed.

Did you pee on your pillow? I say.

Yeah, he says, and he doesn't even look the least bit remorseful, just grins up at me like this is something to be proud of, this peeing on a pillow he'll sleep on soon. It's all I can do to pick him up and take him to the potty instead of throwing all those books across the room in a rage, because it's every single day, *every single day* that I'm battling twins. It's relentless and exhausting and, sometimes, way too much.

We Count it All Joy

I'm already crying on the way back from the potty—from anger or disappointment or despair, I don't know. I put him in his playpen without a word and close the door, because I don't even want to know what happens next. All the way back to my room I can feel the dam breaking, the one that's been piling for too long, the one that ends in *I don't want to be the mother of twins anymore.*

I never asked for twins, and yet, there they are, in the next room, tearing everything apart.

Especially me.

///

It was three months after losing a baby that we got pregnant again.

The baby-losing had left a hole so wide and deep it felt like it could only be filled with a new baby. So when I took that pregnancy test and it said yes, my heart healed the tiniest little bit.

We waited weeks to even go to the doctor, because the last baby had died at nine weeks and we didn't know it until the twelfth week, and I wanted to make sure this one lived before I got my hopes up. Except my hopes flew high the minute I saw a positive test. Tentative and yet solid.

My husband came with me for the first appointment, because I could barely lift my head I was so sick—but mostly because the last appointment, when the screen showed a baby had died, I sat on an examination table alone, and he did not want me to do it again, if this one was not alive. My doctor's nurse practitioner brought that familiar, bulky machine into the bright-white room, and it only took a second to see the two where there had ever been only one. We were shocked and excited and terrified, all sorts of emotions fighting their way to the middle of our hearts.

We had no idea what we were in for.

///

No one does, really, when they're having a baby. Babies are unpredictable beings. But this was different, because there were two. We really had no idea.

No one told us how hard it would be. No one told us there would be days we wished we could give one away, and we knew which one it would be. No one told us there would be whole months where we questioned our ability to keep on keeping on, where someone's *You're such great parents. I don't know how you do it,* would make us burst into tears, because we knew we weren't "doing it." No one told us we'd live with those daily thoughts that sounded a lot like *They're so cute, I'm so lucky I get to have twins, What's cooler than this?* and also like *I give up* and *Someone please take one of them* and *I wish I hadn't had them.*

We kept telling ourselves it would get easier. We believed it, too. After that foggy first year we hardly remember anymore, we told ourselves it would be easier because they would be older and could feed themselves. Except then they were mobile and there were two babies to keep safe and out of things and entertained so they didn't tear the whole house down around us.

There were two drinks to pour and two drinks to keep on trays so they weren't knocked to the floor where they'd make two big puddles of milk we'd have to clean up. There were four hands throwing food on the floor. There were two babies to change and two babies breaking into bathrooms to unravel whole rolls of expensive eco-friendly toilet paper into a now-stopped-up toilet and two babies turning on water faucets so they run for an hour before we even noticed. There were two babies tearing out the pages of books and two babies climbing out of cribs and two babies taking off diapers to play with poop. There were two babies getting into closets and drawers and pulling the stuffing out of stuffed animals and making holes in walls bigger and locking themselves in bathrooms.

Now there's potty training and twice the accidents and twice the frustration and twice the I-just-peed-on-the-floor-because-I-felt-like-it-even-though-I-know-betters, and some days I honestly don't want to do it anymore.

It doesn't get easier the older they get. I know this now. There will always be two of them going through the same developmental stage, and, my God, I did not ask for this.

///

That first night home from the hospital, where they'd spent twenty days in neonatal intensive care for being born six weeks early, we tried assigning a twin to each of us, my husband and me. But then they both woke up at the same time for a feeding, and neither of us got sleep enough to take care of the three other boys who needed us, too.

The next night we parceled out shifts, with one parent taking the 11:30 p.m. and midnight feedings and the other taking the 2:30 and 3 a.m. feedings, and the first parent taking the 5:30 and 6 a.m. feedings. Except we'd start feeding one, and the other would wake up and scream to be fed. They were slow eaters, and the first one would take forty-five minutes to finish three ounces, and the second one would scream for forty-five minutes until he got his food, and neither of us slept, again. Every time I listened to those babies crying, my heart started crying, too, because it was already too too much.

We had tried to avoid it, because I wanted to hold my babies, but we finally, for the sake of sanity, caved to feeding them both at the same time in a swing and spent the rest of that year sticking bottles into mouths and counting down to when feeding time would be over, because we were overwhelmed and exhausted.

And then hard never left.

It didn't take us long to know and understand that nothing about twins would ever, ever be easy.

///

Almost every time we take our twins out in public, at least one person will ask if they're twins, even though they look exactly alike. *Yes*, we'll say, *they're twins*, and it never fails what they'll say next:

So cute. I always wanted twins.

My husband and I will look at each other.

No. You didn't, our eyes will say to each other. *You want the idea of twins, but you don't want twins. Trust us.* But we smile politely and say, yeah, twins are really fun, because they *are* really fun sometimes, and then other times they're maddening and crazy and way too much to manage.

A whole lot of the time they are crazy-makers.

Twins are the hardest challenge I have ever faced in parenting, and I would never wish them upon anyone. It sounds terrible all packaged like that, but it's true.

People also like to tell me all the time that they had kids who were really close together—almost like twins. I have done that, too, with Boy 2 only fourteen months older than Boy 3, but it is not the same as twins. Not the same at all.

My twins beat me and break me and bust me all up inside, and sometimes I don't even know how to handle all the hard they bring to a life. Sometimes I don't even want to.

///

Last spring my brother and sister-in-law announced that they were pregnant with twins. I felt excited for them, of course, because they'd waited so long to have a baby, just one. But I also felt afraid, because I know how tough twins are, how tempers can fly and anger can follow one in and out of rooms for days on end, without explanation.

I knew that there are days when you feel strung so tight you know you can't take one more thing because of the ringer your twins wrapped you around this morning, and then you'll open a door to walls and a floor and two babies, who were supposed to be sleeping all this time, covered in poop. And there are days when you think it might be getting easier, and then a twin climbs over the gate barring the upstairs and pulls down half the books in the library before you can get to him, and you're so busy picking up all those books you forget there's another unsupervised one downstairs, and before you can make it back down, he's pulled out the entire economy package of four hundred Band Aids and stuck them all to the bathroom floor. And there are days when one will run out the back door without shoes and you're trying to chase him to get those shoes on and the other one will see his chance and run out the front door someone forgot to barricade-lock, and he's halfway down the street before you even notice he's gone.

There are days when, for a split second, you wonder if you should just let him go.

I couldn't very well tell them all this, though, so I voiced my congratulations and then encouraged them to find help. I took pictures of poop walls and emptied-onto-the-floor closets so we could laugh about all those twinanigans that happen every other minute of a day and race a parent toward breakdown.

The day before Father's Day, my sister-in-law went into

labor twenty weeks early, and doctors couldn't stop it, and she delivered them, two boys, and held them and watched them claw for breath they could not find because they had only the tiniest beginnings of lungs. And then she watched them die.

That night, I hugged my two babies a little tighter.

///

I know what a blessing every child is. I do.

I know what it's like to lose a baby. I have.

I know how it feels to watch a child fall so sick he might die. He almost did.

I know what it's like. I know.

I know the incredible gift of five healthy boys, the gift of another on the way, the gift of a home filled with wild, untamable boys. And I remember it all when they're finally asleep and I can breathe again.

It's just that during those waking moments, when a twin is pulling everything in sight off a counter because I haven't had time to put away what his brothers stacked there, and another twin has found the pencil his older brother used for homework and is now marking all over the pages of a library book, I forget. There is not enough of me, and I forget.

I forget that one twin's name means "swift and honorable," how one day he will be strong and solid and mighty, how he is all of that now, bundled in a sometimes-unmanageable two-year-old boy. I forget that the other twin's name means "God remembers," because he was a gift in the losing, two blessings that took away the one curse, how he shows love's nature in his very being. He is all of this now, bundled in a sometimes-difficult two-year-old boy. And even though mothering twins may be the hardest parenting challenge I've ever been given to date, I know, too, that they are tearing me apart every single minute of every single day.

They are the ones who pull those words from my lips: *I just can't do this life anymore.*

This is a good place to be, I think—because it's only when we can't do this life anymore that we give an inch more to Another who can do it much better for us. *I can't do it* is another door into surrender.

I can choose to raise these twins all on my own power and patience, and I will fail every time. Or I can choose to raise them on the power and patience of Another. I can drink from the well that will never run dry, and I will see victory every time.

I know what happens when I choose my own, limited power and patience. I think about how nice it would be to give one away, or I wish I hadn't had them, or I see in a clouded way that covers all the sunshine they've brought into a mama life. Double laughter. Double joy. Double love, not just double trouble.

Clear eyes can see it better than clouded ones. So this day, I choose to see.

On How Children Heal the Father Wound

I am one of the fatherless ones.

According to the statistics, I should have turned my angst toward drugs. I should have run with the racy crowd. I should have dropped out of school and skipped college altogether and raised my parcel of kids on my own. Instead, I graduated at the top of my class and then became a first-generation college graduate and then married young and had a parcel of kids I would raise with an amazing, loving, creative, one-of-a-kind man.

But all those accomplishments don't mean I escaped without deep-seated scars and a lifetime of insecurity and a wounded heart that bled at the slightest puncture. I got all of this, too. And those scars and insecurities and the wounded heart showed up in things like anorexia and bulimia and perfectionism and isolation and fear and anxiety that chased me through whole days and weeks and months but did not yet have a name.

Then something miraculous happened. Babies began to slip into my world, and I began to find all my missing pieces. I began to heal.

This was unexpected. It was extraordinary.

It is one of the loveliest parts of the mother journey.

///

It all began nine years ago, when a Valentine's Day pregnancy test told me what I wanted and feared most: there would be a baby. I was young, just two years married to my husband. My battle with eating disorders felt too near, and the self-image insecurities hid just beneath the surface of an ever-rising scale.

It was hard to watch those numbers adding up over days and weeks and months, hard to watch a belly rounding, even though it held a precious treasure. I'd worked so obsessively to make it stay flat. It was hard not to think about what that belly might look like later, after a baby no longer hid inside it, because looks were still important. Skinny still equaled beautiful, and maybe I could be beautiful now, pregnant, with a belly swelling around new life, but would I be beautiful later?

And then he was here on a cold evening in November, and he locked eyes with me, and his held words my husband had tried to say, over and over and over again: *You are loved because you are you. And the you you are is beautiful.*

So all those days after, when people brought meals and I tried to count calories, sometimes not eating at all, and I logged eight-mile runs every day, trying so desperately to get my figure back, I had only to pick up my baby and look into those eyes so aware, so intelligent even then, so indiscriminately loving from the very beginning, to know the truth: beauty does not live in a body but in a heart. And he would grow and show me in a million more ways these eight years he's been mine—in pictures he'd snap with an old camera, "just because you're beautiful," even though I was still in pajamas and didn't have on any makeup; in that knock on our bedroom door when we've closed up for the night, just because "I forgot to give you another kiss;" in the smile he wears when I dress up for a date with his daddy.

It took the eyes of a child to show me how beautiful a woman could be, in her love for a child.

And so these days after having another baby, these days when a stomach needs shrinking once more and it takes more time because it's the fifth time, I don't worry or stress or obsess like I would have done all those years ago. I know I am loved for more than mere beauty.

And I know I am beautiful simply because I am me.

///

The second one met me with a compassionate heart and his daddy's blue eyes and all those emotions that took us by storm when his brother felt hurt or when he felt alone or when he accidentally broke something that was important to him or someone else, like the blue paper monster named Xerxes his brother was making.

He burned all my bridges down.

Every time tears turned blue eyes to glass, I heard the

voice from my past:
I'll give you something to cry about.
Big girls don't cry.
You're weak like her if you cry about something as silly as this.

Something as silly as someone else's dog getting run over or a handicapped child unable to cross the street by himself or an old man out to dinner alone, still wearing his wedding ring.

I looked at my sweet boy with his so sweet heart, and I called that voice's bluff—because I learned from a little boy the beauty of emotion, the way feelings can heal a broken world, how tears can wet a dry ground and bring forth something new and green and marvelous, how big emotions can walk us deeper into life. And every time I reached my arms out to my cares-a-whole-lot-about-everything boy, I felt those pieces of my soul shift and the empty spaces fill—because he was me and I was him, and the emotion was a gift, not a curse like I had been told when I was a girl.

I could cry without shame. I could hope without disappointment. I could love with abandon.

I could live.

///

The third son slid into our lives on a late afternoon in July, and he had the eyes of the first and the heart of the second and a lion's share of courage and daring and trust. All those growing days he was the little brother who wanted to be exactly like his bigger brothers, so he flipped off couches at eighteen months old and hung upside down off monkey bars when he was two and jumped off moving swings when he was three, and I watched it all with trepidation mixed with hope, because he, too, was finding pieces of my soul that had gone missing.

Mine had been a forced courage all my life, a measured courage that only tried what I knew I'd be good at, because failure always waited for that one little mistake, that one not-quite, that one whoops, and if I failed, who would I be then? I would not be a daughter they could be proud of or a wife he could be proud of or a mother they could be proud of.

And then I watched my daring, courageous, firecracker-of-a-boy try that bike without training wheels when he was too young for a bike without training wheels, and I watched him wobble and lose control and fall and then get right back on and do it again. I watched him try a back flip on the trampoline and land on his knees instead of his feet and get right back up and do it again. I watched him propel himself from the height of a swing so he flew for one second in time, and he slipped all the way down the hill and landed on his behind and giggled about it before getting back up and doing it again.

It took the bravery of a four-year-old to show me that trying and failing and trying again, in spite of the failure, is the real test of courage, not doing only what we know we've already mastered. He was still loved, even though he had failed.

I could fail, and it would not change how much I was loved. I could fail, and it would not change who I was. I could fail, and it would make me stronger.

///

The fourth and fifth came to us in late March, and they spent twenty days in the neonatal intensive care unit, testing the will and patience and trust of a mama and daddy almost to its breaking point. And then they came home and life blurred, the whole year flashing by without our really knowing what was happening. We could do this, and we would prove it.

Then they turned two and stripped our self-sufficiency right off the skin of our backs, and people came to us from our amazing community, offering their help. The desperation answered for us: *Yes. Please. Anything you want to do to help.*

All my life I'd pushed away the help of others, because I could do life myself, alone, and if I couldn't, then it was failure. It was not enough. It was shame on you.

Two babies changed it all. Because we needed help from the people who came to sit with three so we could visit the other two stuck at the hospital. We needed help from those couples who offered their presence so a strung-tight mama and daddy could have a few hours away, a date of sorts. We needed help from everyone who gave us extra baby clothes and gift cards for baby things and casseroles stacked on refrigerator shelves. Our babies did not care that we needed help or that we couldn't do it on our own. They loved and lived. We did, too.

It took the acceptance of two little boys to help me see it clearly: asking for help was not weakness, a deficiency that proved our mistake in having so many. It was strength, because we are all in this life together. We all march on, together.

I was not alone, ever. Not even in this.

///

And now, this last baby, who slid into the world the day before my birthday. He has healed a heart, too, already, in his eighteen days of living—because there was a birthday morning and evening and night when he looked into my eyes and handed me another missing piece.

You see, I've never had a great relationship with birthdays, not just because of the getting older, but because, too, every birthday of my childhood I waited on a call that did not come, from one I still loved even though he'd left. And this year on my birthday I sat in a hospital bed, eight hours after delivering another beautiful boy, and I held my boy and kissed his lips and forgot all about that call. Here was a tiny piece of perfection, and it was all I ever needed in this world.

Those birthdays used to come and go, and the silence spoke of another silence, of another Father who probably didn't remember my birthday, either. Except there was this: a boy born to me safe and healthy and ALIVE, even though we had wondered and worried about the alive part of it, because of a condition I developed in my liver this time around. A condition that might cause stillbirth.

The day before my birthday, the day of my birthday, the day after my birthday, I held a precious, costly gift, and he was ALIVE, and he stared at me and I stared at him, and I heard words that he could not speak and yet could, because a soul can connect and speak to another soul.

You have never been forgotten. You see? That's what the voice said.

And I did see. I saw a tiny hand on a breast. I saw eyes that might stay blue blinking hard and then fluttering into the peaceful sleep of a newborn on a mama's chest. I saw beauty and perfection and love in the rise and fall of a tiny belly, in the silk of a rounded cheek, in the cute curve of a nose.

I saw the love of a Father who could give new life in the hours before a birthday.

It took the presence of a newborn to remind me that I have never, not in the hardest of all my years, been forgotten. And every year on the day that is my birthday linked to his, I will remember.

///

I did not know they would do this. I did not know the exhausting-yet-precious presence of six boys would heal me in the ways I have been healed. But they certainly have.

There is a miracle in motherhood: that we become exactly who we were created to be in all their chafing and stretching and rounding off of our edges so we can see a world and ourselves more clearly. It's unexpected. It's startling. It's hard and intense and humbling.

And there is nothing more beautiful in all the world.

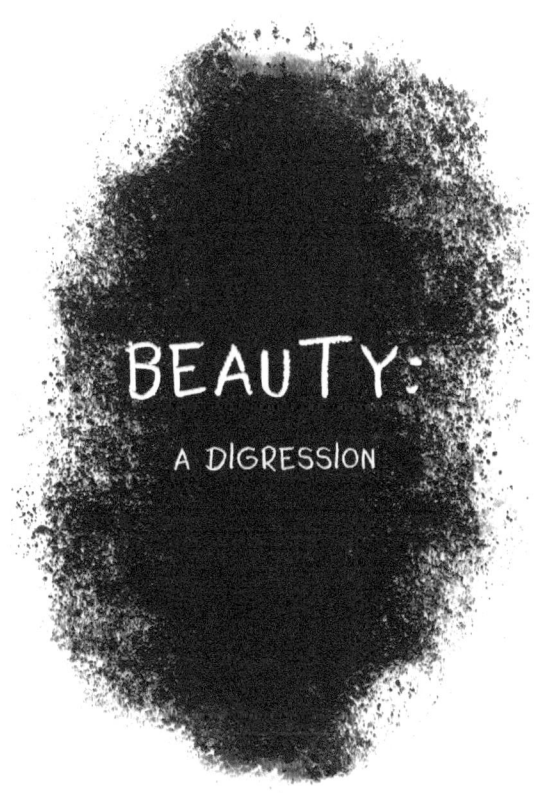

On the Sexualization of Women

We sit on the bed, watching the fifth episode of the first season of *Game of Thrones*, and I'm waiting for the scenes where we will turn our faces away, because they always come. We recently started watching this series last weekend, because I've read all the books and loved the story and was curious about this show we've heard so much about. The kids were with grandparents for our anniversary and we had the time, so we checked out a copy at the library and sat back to enjoy. After a few episodes I said to my husband, *I think they have a contract to show boobs and sex at least once in every episode.*

And we laugh about it again tonight, because we're nearing the end of an episode that only showed a woman's naked body twice, which feels like progress at this point, but if I'm really being honest, twice or ten times, it all bothers me the same. I start wondering what these women had to do during the audition for a show like this one. Did they have to walk the room naked, to prove they had the right kind of breasts and bodies that didn't jiggle too much and a backside that screamed beauty and desire and perfection all at the same time? And what about the ones who didn't have those perfect bodies, because one breast was a little smaller than the other or they had a little more stomach movement than another actress or they, God forbid, wanted the part but weren't comfortable showing the "necessary" pieces?

What kind of screening process happened here for a show like *Game of Thrones*, and how in the world does this help rather than hurt all those glaring societal problems—girls starving themselves to death, young women believing they don't have the body they need to make it in this world, mothers walking around searching for their worth because their waistline isn't as defined as it should be and their hips aren't as narrow as they need to be and their breasts sag a little more than they should because they've carried and birthed and fed babies? How does it help rather than hurt all the deeper issues, like sexism and pornography and the sex slave trade?

We can deny that these things have anything to do with each other, but we have only to scratch the surface of a world and its progressive sexuality to know that they do. The sexual content warning in a show or movie used to mean a man with his shirt off and a woman in a bra or under covers or in a cloudy shower. Now it means a man with his shirt off and a woman showing her naked breasts or likely more.

More and more shows and movies and print and broadcast mediums are picking up on this trend, so women are constantly sexualized and demeaned and disrespected, their worth tied to their bodies. What can we do about it? Do we even want to do something about it? Because, for these women, it's a job, and who are we to complain about money and the earning power that comes from baring a body?

///

I was a freshman in high school when I discovered something was wrong with my body. Those girls, my classmates and teammates, would walk around the locker room naked, on their way to the showers after a sweaty volleyball practice, and I couldn't help but notice they didn't look like me.

So I'd pull a towel around my own body before I undressed, stripping my clothes beneath the cover of a tiny white piece of terrycloth, and I wore my protection all the way to the shower and waited until I'd closed the curtain and made sure there were no gaps someone could accidentally see through before I peeled it away. There was nowhere to hang that towel except on two walls or the curtain rod, all places where water would soak it, so I wouldn't even dry when finished. I would just wrap the wet towel back around my body and walk back to my cubby with my head down. Then I'd try to wiggle into all my clothes before I pulled the towel away again.

A wet towel was preferable to showing a body that didn't have perfect boobs like one girl or a flat stomach like another one or a tight, bubbly backside like her. They all looked like the girls I saw in magazines, but me, well, I needed a whole lot of work.

My insecurity followed me into adulthood, and it kept me "pure," but it kept me chained, too.

///

We were experimental on our anniversary, those three days without children, eating at restaurants we'd never tried and visiting places around town we'd never been and watching a new show. One night I wanted to eat at a pub, because we'd never done it. So we searched for pubs near our part of town and came up with two, a London one and an Irish one.

We chose the London one because when we pulled up both their web sites, the Irish one showed women with deep cleavage on the home page, like that was the reason we should come. We thought maybe the London pub would be classier. Except we got there, and I looked around, and the waitresses wore short skirts that showed the wrong cheeks when they bent over to hand someone a drink at another table and deep V-necks that showed most of the underneath when they set our own drinks down.

After the initial discomfort, I felt all the familiar emotions come dripping in. Sadness. Anger. Confusion. How do these women apply for a job? Do they have to show they have nice legs and enough cleavage to please a looking customer? Do they have to sign an agreement to do what it takes, leave as little to the imagination as possible, to make a few extra bucks?

All around the room were couples, but here and there were tables of men, and those were the tables where waitresses hung out. Was that a requirement of the job, too? Be flirty. Show what you have. Excite the men, especially the ones without a date.

What the hell are we doing?

We rant and moan about how women, after all these years, are still inferior to their male counterparts, how we're not taken seriously in the workforce, how we live in a world where women are more conquests and trophies and posters than anything else, and there are places like this that exist in our cities? We talk about how we need workplace reform, but how does that even become a possibility in a society that believes the slang word for women's breasts is an acceptable name for a mainstream restaurant as long as the logo looks more like owl eyes? We live in a world where body shapes and bust sizes and perfectly round behinds can get us a job anywhere, if we're the right kind of woman, and, because of it, all women lose.

///

There was a short window of time when I considered broadcast journalism over print journalism as my career focus. I loved to write and I loved telling stories, but I loved the thought of being on television, too. I wanted to be someone like Barbara Walters, making a difference in the world.

I talked about it with a friend, who had chosen broadcast as her focus, and she said the words that made my decision for me: *You have a good face,* she said. And then she elbowed me and grinned. *But you might have to show a little cleavage.*

Because even in the media world, we, the women, weren't safe.

It was bad enough that we had to have the right face, when this was not a requirement of the men who sat behind a camera beside us. We needed more than just our faces to prove our worth in a media world.

So, instead, I buried myself in print journalism, where no one had to see my face or my body to judge how good I was. I convinced myself I could be safe here.

///

But we're not safe anywhere, not really. There are shows where a man's naked parts are never shown but women's parts are. And there are restaurants where men are not asked to be flirty and sexual, but women are. And there are no age limits on a man's longevity in media or theater or modeling, but there are for women.

Sure, a woman's body is beautiful, but every time we ask her—or require her—to bare those sacred pieces, give them away to millions of viewers or patrons, she loses something, and we are taking it. Dignity. Significance. Worth. No woman can show those pieces of herself and be the same. No man can see those pieces she shows and be the same.

We talk about the need for women to boycott films like *Fifty Shades of Grey* and *Magic Mike* (never saw either) to take a stand against pornography, but just look at the ways we are allowing Hollywood to sexualize women and anesthetize men to all the soft porn that flies through their eyes every single day—through television and billboards and movies and restaurants around our cities. If we are not taking a stand in these tiny little places, we will not win the war over pornography, and we will not change the way our daughters and wives and sisters see their own bodies, and we will just be spinning our proverbial wheels along this road toward gender equality.

A woman sexualized is a woman who cannot be respected for who she really is. A woman sexualized is a woman whose work will be limited in the world, depending on how she looks. A woman sexualized is a woman who will never break past the ceiling of a man's world.

Does this mean we stay away from those restaurants, even though their food is good? Does it mean we stop watching that show, even though we like the story? Does it mean we tell our real truth on those restaurant opinion cards and try to lobby for greater accountability in Hollywood and speak out everywhere we can?

I don't claim to know all the answers. I don't even claim to have the right one. I only know that we have much work to do.

///

I had already stopped eating years before, but my first year of college, when all those others were gaining their freshman fifteen, I was losing my freshman thirty.

My scholarship paid for a full meal plan—breakfast, lunch and dinner—but I didn't bother with details like that. Some days I just swiped my card for a smoothie and let that be my nourishment for the day. Some days I splurged on a bagel, too. Most days I didn't eat at all.

Every single day, no matter how tired or weak or busy, I showed up at the student workout facility and ran six miles and lifted weights and worked on my core that never seemed to shape up the way I wanted it to. I ran to the practice football field where the college marching band practiced, and I worked hard through two hours of grueling marching, and then I ran all the way back to my dorm. I walked everywhere I went.

One day my roommate watched me try to cinch a new belt tight enough, but I'd run out of holes, and she said, *You're getting too skinny.* She dragged me to the dining hall that night and piled my plate high with pizza and enchiladas and rice and bread, and then she sat me down and stood over me and said, *Eat.*

And I did, but she couldn't save me. That's the night I started throwing up what I had eaten.

It was a sick cycle, that trying to be beautiful and never quite getting there. The boy I had my sights on, a cute baseball player with evening sky eyes, kept me around as a friend so I could hang out with all those other baseball players who needed free algebra tutoring. I'd hear them talk about those other girls with their legs and their "racks" and the tanned skin, but never their faces or their brains, which was all I really had going for me. I'd leave those tutoring sessions thinking, *I will never be hot enough to make it in this world.*

But I didn't stop trying—starving and bingeing and purging and working out every second I had a chance—because society and the men I knew and all those images in the media told me I needed to be something I was not, and I had to figure out a way to do it.

Like every woman does.

///

It's gotten better as the years have stretched on and babies have stretched skin and faith has stretched eyes to see what matters most. But in my weakest moments, I still try to figure out a way to do it. A way to lose the rest of this baby weight. A way to ensure I don't gain much in a new pregnancy. A way to hear them say, *I can't believe she's had six babies.* And I've heard them say it, too, and I've felt the victory spread all through my veins, and I always feel just a little bit sad when it does, because I still, after all this time, believe that a body tells the story of who I am.

Movies and media and these restaurants around town don't help.

What will happen to these women when they have babies, when they grow too old, when they lose the elasticity and firmness and beauty that got them these jobs in their younger years and they bared a body on a screen or in a magazine or walking around a food establishment?

I don't know. Maybe they'll be okay. Maybe they won't.

But I do believe that we won't completely heal these jagged places in a woman's world until we start protecting what needs protecting, until we demand our dignity back, until we look for ways to tell our story with a body covered instead of bared. And we can't do it alone. We need our husbands and our brothers and our fathers protecting and demanding and telling, too.

Those issues are all tangled up around each other—the body image issues and the pornography issues and the slavery issues. There is not one problem but many. There is not one answer to all those why-questions but many. There is not one solution but many. I hope we can be brave enough to tackle as many problems and try out as many solutions as we can for as long as it takes.

I believe change is necessary, and I believe it's possible. And maybe that's as good enough a place to start as any.

On Pregnancy and Body Image

It happened just a few days ago, during the greeting time at church, when a woman I've known for years hugged my neck and kissed my cheek and then said, *You look so beautiful.*

I managed to hold back my laugh, but I couldn't stop words from sliding out after hers. *I sure don't feel beautiful.*

We never do, she said, and she smiled and walked back to the seat beside her husband.

Those words. They have chased me since.

We never do, do we? We who are carrying the beauty of new life, we who are right here in the middle of backs aching and stomachs stretching and clothes cutting into places they shouldn't be, because they're supposed to be made for this—we are not often the first ones to say we feel beautiful. We feel lumbering and awkward and swollen and heavy and achy and frumpy and all those things that disqualify us from beautiful.

It took everything I had today to put on those getting-uncomfortable stretchy jeans instead of the yoga pants I wear almost every day. It took everything I had to pull on a form-fitting green-sleeved maternity shirt that shows the round ball throwing off my center of gravity, instead of hiding behind an oversized T-shirt I stole from my husband's side of the closet. And even though I made this great effort, I feel anything but beautiful.

This makes me feel sad.

///

I never really wanted to have children. I was young when I became aware of my body, comparing it to others and noticing the differences. I was never as thin or as strong or as beautiful as I wanted and needed to be, according to beauty magazines. I worked hard to measure up. I watched what I ate and started skipping meals and made bargains with myself before I even knew what it all meant, before I knew how it would lock me in chains.

If I can just be as small as her…

If I can just get a stomach like hers…

If I can just fit into the same size she wears…

And then I got older, and I watched high school girls in grades ahead and grades below swell with unplanned babies, and I never wanted to be them. I would never lose my body like that, I said.

I wrote it in my journal.

I told my mom.

I whispered it in the dark hours of the night, when I thought of the hips I already hated and the stomach I had to practically kill myself to make flat and the arms that required half an hour every day to stay cut.

And then I met my husband. We were married two

years, and the longing to start a family came knocking. I almost said no, because I was the thinnest I'd ever been and I finally felt good and strong and almost maybe beautiful. But then I missed a period, and I took a pregnancy test and three more just to be sure. And then I sat in a bathroom and cried over the plus signs lined up on the counter.

I cried because I was happy, because I would be a mother. I cried because I was terrified, because I would be a mother. I cried because somewhere along the way beauty had become tangled around thin. Skinny. Hot body.

Those plus signs told me I was losing something, too, and I didn't know how to reconcile the loss.

///

When I've talked with people about body image, about the eating disorders of my past and the still-present constant striving to always be thinner and the way that crooked desire never really leaves us, I often tell them that the struggle seemed to get better with children. But the way I feel today, with ten weeks left on the new-baby countdown, I can't say it's completely true.

I stopped looking at myself in the mirror five weeks ago. I don't care to see the way my belly has stretched so thin there are veins and shimmery stretch marks running up and down my skin so it all looks papery and bluish and bruised. I don't care to see the varicose vein that just showed up on the back of my left knee two weeks ago, the one I thought might be a blood clot but is, instead, a "normal" part of pregnancy. I don't care to see the fuller face staring back at me.

Every time I feel that pinch in the middle of my back, I feel unbeautiful. Every time I feel hungry enough to eat, even though I just ate an hour ago, I feel unbeautiful. Every time I step on a scale and see all the pounds added, I feel unbeautiful.

So I stand in front of a TV screen and gasp through pregnancy interval training. I bend my body into positions that hurt like hell during prenatal yoga. I speed walk until I'm breathing too hard and sweating too much and my back is screaming, because I have to log at least thirty minutes of exercise before I'll let myself quit.

I try to pretend their good-natured jokes and comments don't hit me right where it hurts: "They're sure it's not twins, right?" "Sure one isn't hiding?" "Wow, you got big fast. Twins again?"

Here I am, in my last pregnancy, and I cannot just let myself be pregnant. Why can't I just let myself be pregnant?

The real truth is, pregnancy does not heal something like this. Sometimes it only makes it worse.

///

I blew up in my first pregnancy. Forty pounds added to my frame over those nine months, and then he was born and I still had twenty-five to lose. They were just numbers, but they were everything to me.

I hated my after-pregnancy body, where jeans I'd worn for years didn't fit right anymore, all tight in the hips and butt and thighs. But I worked hard to lose all the extra weight within the first six weeks. I started to feel better about myself. And then came number two, and five months after him we were pregnant with the third, and I lost track of all the weight I needed to lose to make my pre-pregnancy goal again.

Then came the fourth pregnancy, when I was five pounds from reaching my goal, and I knew I didn't want to blow up like I had for all the others, so I counted calories and kept running and told myself if I could keep from breaking out the maternity clothes in the first fourteen weeks, it would be some kind of victory. Except week eleven started creeping closer, and those pants were getting tighter and tighter, and I stressed and worried and worked all the harder.

I walked into the doctor's office for that finally-made-it-to-the-safe-point appointment, and the scale hadn't changed, and I felt a small victory that only showed in my smile. And then they looked for her heartbeat, the same one I'd heard four weeks ago, and it was gone.

It took me a long time to forgive myself for that little celebration I felt in my heart, for the no weight gain that really only meant a baby had died. It felt all wrong, the way I'd obsessed over weight and worked so hard and kept to my don't-gain-too-much plan, the way I'd cared more about maintaining a body than embracing and growing a baby.

I would never, ever do it again.

///

And yet, here we are, in this place where my husband asks a simple question, *Are you hungry?* and my brain goes to war.

No.

Yes.

No, no, no.

But yes. Yes. So hungry.

I really tried to enjoy it this time around, because this baby is the last one who will need room in my womb, the last one who will keep me from sleeping in these weeks before meeting him, the last one who will stretch me in all these ways I can see and the ones I cannot. But still I felt that touch of relief when I spent fourteen weeks too sick to eat, and the scale dropped. Still I felt glad when a stomach virus knocked me out for three days and the scale dropped more. Still I felt victorious when I reached the halfway point and the file showed no weight gain at all.

I know better than to let a number on a scale define me. I do. It's just that, even now, I can feel its haunting in my knees carrying all this extra weight and my back arching in unnatural ways and the stomach muscles I can't even see anymore. I've made my after-baby lose-the-weight plan, and I am counting down the days until I can get started.

I want to be the woman "they" all point to and say, *I*

can't believe that body has had six babies. Because it's a badge. Or something like that. Because beauty, even after all these years, is still tangled around thin.

And I just want to be beautiful again.

///

Three months after the baby-losing we got pregnant with twins. Ten weeks in I woke from a nap and went to the bathroom. Blood dropped out in a great gush.

I sat on the toilet while my husband ran to the corner store, because we were on our anniversary vacation and I hadn't thought to bring anything with me, since I was pregnant. Then he rushed me to the hospital while I cried beside him because I thought we'd lost two more.

I had a blood clot, caught between my uterus and the placental wall, and no doctor could tell me if my babies were safe, because there was no knowing.

They sent me home on bed rest. I spent seven months on bed rest. I could not even walk for exercise, because no one knew what might tear the placenta more.

And I did it. Because I could not lose another baby.

I didn't worry about my weight, even though the pressure sat right behind my eyes, where it always sits when I try not to think about it.

It took me two years after having twins, two years of intense interval training and three-minute planks and four miles of running every other morning, to finally reach a place where I was even close to my pre-pregnancy goal.

I would never do that again, either.

///

So here we are. Here we are in a place where I can hardly eat without feeling guilty, where I work too hard to stay fit, where I cannot even look in a mirror without feeling anxiety creep into the back of my throat. Here we are in a place that feels anything but beautiful.

What is it about this time, when new life is demanding room, that makes it so hard to believe our swelling skin and fuller face and sturdier legs are all beautiful? What is it about these last few weeks, when we can barely walk without pain twisting in a back or a leg or our feet, that make it so hard to feel beautiful? What is it about those first six postpartum weeks before a doctor signs off on the safety of exercise, when our skin feels flabby and disappointing and maybe even destroyed, that make it so hard to believe that new mother is the most beautiful skin we can wear?

We look around at all those other pregnant women, and we wish we could be them, because we bet their scale hasn't reached the number ours has, and they're so much cuter pregnant than we are, and they'll probably drop the weight in no time, while we'll have to struggle along for years.

It's not easy to feel beautiful when we know about the stretch marks we work hard to hide. We know just how many pounds we've added. We can't help but compare what we have with what those magazine mothers have.

Maybe we won't always feel beautiful. Maybe that's not even the point. Maybe we just have to know that WE ARE.

We are not exempt from this body image struggle, the one that has chased us all our lives, just because our body is being used to create new life. But we can choose to turn our backs on its voice.

So today, when a little girl, not more than four years old, comes up to me at my boys' school and says, *Do you have a baby in your belly?* and I say, *Yes I do,* and she says, *You're so beautiful,* I choose to believe her.

We are beautiful. We are beautiful with our big bellies and our shiny jagged lines in the hidden places and our clothes that have stopped fitting. We are beautiful with our increasing scale number and our puffy didn't-sleep-last-night eyes and our feet too swollen to even wear shoes at this point.

We are beautiful with our new life.

Believe it. Know it. And then live into it.

On Beauty

Some days I know the truth, and some days it gets buried so far beneath those old lies I can hardly remember its echo.

This morning I woke up feeling out of sorts. Not unexpected, since there is a baby who had trouble sleeping. Since there was a brain that just wouldn't turn off. Since there is work that has, lately, followed me right into sleep.

But this was something different. Something deeper.

This was me. This was my body. This was lie, a pair of them, rising up from the graveyard, where I thought I'd buried them long, long ago.

You see, I wrote an article about a woman's body after pregnancy that got a whole lot of attention, and here came all those haters, hating. Their voices stirred those ghosts from their graves. While I was sleeping, the corpses came walking, and when I looked in the mirror this morning, they opened their mouths to speak.

Six weeks you've had, they said. *Six weeks you've had to lose that belly. AND IT IS STILL HERE.*

And then they smiled with their rotten teeth and told me the worst part of it all: *Unbeautiful. This is unbeautiful. You are unbeautiful.*

I could not argue. Not right now. Not today. Because today, this moment, their words feel true.

///

The first time I heard their voices, I was too young to know them for what they were. I listened to commercials and all those teen magazines and the Hollywood ideal of thin and pretty, and I stopped eating lunch when I was twelve. I stopped eating breakfast when I was a freshman in high school. I stopped eating the last meal of the day my first day of college, because, for the first time in my life, there was no one to monitor what I ate or didn't eat.

I thought I could get away with it and that I would finally reach my target weight, which was bony and completely and utterly fatless. But I had a roommate who cared. She noticed my rapidly dropping weight and dragged me to dinner at a dining hall every chance she got. So it wasn't long before I started purging those suppers.

I would walk with her to the dining hall and eat whatever I wanted, and then, when she was preoccupied with our friends across the hall, I would slip off to the bathroom and do what needed to be done. When she noticed, I made my excuses. Something I ate made me sick. Stress. A virus, maybe. She didn't buy it, so the next stop was laxatives, because that was easier to hide. It was my course load, the pressure to make good grades, the stressful news job that kept me in the bathroom all the time. Laxatives got me through the rest of that semester.

Bulimia never really had my heart, though. I much preferred anorexia. So as soon as I moved off campus, I returned to the familiar hunger pains. I kept cans of green beans in the pantry, and the days I felt especially hungry, I'd allow myself one can a day. My roommates were too busy to notice.

Then I met my husband, and there came a night when he left a note on my computer at the newspaper office.

Skinny does not equal beautiful, it said. And for some reason, I almost believed him.

I looked at that note every time I sat down in my office chair and every time I got up to leave. It rescued me before my heart could stop from the sickness, but there are other ways to die than the physical ones, and I was already well on my way, gripped by the compulsive claws of anorexia.

///

Today is a reckoning day, six weeks postpartum, a day when I will visit my doctor again and stand on that scale. A scale that will tell me how much I have left to lose. A scale that will tell me, just a little bit, who I am now.

I hate that this is so. All this time I've stayed away from the scale, because I said it didn't matter, and I meant it this time. I really did. This son is my last baby, and I just wanted to enjoy him without worrying about what I look like. And that's exactly what I did. Until now.

I dressed for the morning. Those after-pregnancy transition jeans fit. A transition shirt hid the pooch. I got

We Count it All Joy

my hopes up, I guess.

And then I walk in the doctor's office and I step on the scale and I see how much weight is left, and I crumble. I thought it would be different, not as quite much, not quite as ugly. Those voices start their howling.

Guess you should have tried harder, they say.

Guess you should have exercised more, they say.

Guess you should have worried about it a little more, instead of indulging in your son, they say.

I try to swallow the disappointment, and then the nurse takes me to a room with a mirror, and I have to look at my body before I wrap a flimsy sheet of paper around it, and I can't help it. I turn away, because I don't want to look. I know what's there. Sagging skin that may or may not shrink back this time, because this is the sixth time. Lines that mark my midsection and a belly button that's hardly even a belly button anymore it's been stretched and pulled and rearranged so often.

Those voices grab all of it and fling it right back in my face. Right back in my heart.

This is what unbeautiful feels like.

///

Just after the first was born, I did not know how a woman's body worked. So when he slid out and my belly turned to mush, I cried. It wasn't supposed to be like this. I wasn't supposed to look like this.

Our first day home from the hospital, when my body

had only spent thirty-six hours recovering from a thirteen-hour labor, I went for a walk, because exercise has always been my crutch. Three weeks after he was born, I was out running, with a uterus that hadn't even fully shrunk and hips that were only just sliding back into place and joints that couldn't really take the jarring pressure of five miles. I didn't care. I pushed it anyway.

When I injured myself, because my body wasn't ready for what I was demanding of it, I quit eating. I pretended I wasn't hungry. I let my husband consume those meals people so kindly dropped by.

And then one day he shook me by the shoulders. *You have to eat,* he said. *This isn't the way to do it.*

I knew he was right. But it was so hard. So hard. Because every time I looked in the mirror, what I saw was unbeautiful.

Anorexia makes it hard to see anything else.

///

So this is what unbeautiful feels like.

It feels sad and sharp and hard and achy and impossible and shocking. Most of all it is shocking.

We can go whole years knowing and believing and living the truth, and then one thing, *one tiny little thing,* can raise the dead and make them walk again. It happens for many reasons, this feeling unbeautiful. It happens because someone drops an insensitive comment about our bodies that hits us right where it hurts. It happens because we live in a society that tells us skinny equals beautiful and don't you dare argue. It happens because we look in the mirror and the body looking back is not the one we think we need or want.

Unbeautiful, the kind that makes us starve or cut and bleed or stick a finger down our throat—it is a sickness. An addiction. A compulsion. There is no real cure, at least not one that will last forever. There is only one day at a time.

Every day we are offered the choice to look in the mirror and shake our fists at those living-again lies and say: *No. I don't believe you. This body is not unbeautiful. It is strong. It is amazing. It is the loveliest beautiful there ever, ever was.* Because this is the truth.

Or we can believe the lies. Believing the lies locks us into our harmful patterns of skip the food, binge and purge, count calories to the utmost accuracy.

I want to embrace the truth.

So after my doctor finishes her examination and releases me and walks from the room, I return to the mirror, and I dress again and then snap a picture, because I want to remember. I want to remember the day I looked at my body and finally, finally, finally said out loud, if only to myself, what was true: *This body. I am so very proud of what it has done. It has housed and carried and nourished six boys and a girl we will meet in glory. So what if there is still an after-belly six weeks later?* THIS BODY HAS DONE SOMETHING AMAZING AND BEAUTIFUL. *It needs to revel in that. So I will let it take its time.*

And I mean it.

Those corpses, the anorexia and bulimia that have breathed down my neck all morning, start crawling back to their graves, because you know what? They know, too.

This is what beautiful feels like.

On Birthdays

Time has been holding my hand these last few weeks.

Not in the way of an intimate friend, but in the way of an impatient parent trying to drag a slow-to-get-ready-child out the door so they won't be late.

It's not the last stage of pregnancy that makes me feel so brittle and bruised. Not really. It's the birthday coming up that I don't want to mark, because I don't like marking my climbing age anymore.

I know I can't possibly always have seen birthdays like this, because I was a really young child once, and every really young child dreams of growing up someday. But for as long as I can remember, I have hated growing older.

It's not the birthdays, exactly. It's their number, the way they creep around every year, the way they whisper things like *time is running out* and *you haven't done enough with the years you've been given* and *you should be farther along the writer path than you are today.*

Birthdays, for a long time now, have looked down on me in disappointment, tallying up those years and stretching their hand across all my past, as if to say, *This is all there is?*

Yes. This is all there is. I wanted it to be more, but time

was never exactly kind, and days rushed toward dark, and weeks ran toward months, and whole years, when I didn't really know what I was doing or where I was going or who I even was, slipped right through my fingers.

///

I don't know exactly when those birthdays began breathing down my neck. Maybe it was the ninth one, when I blew out candles on a ballerina cake my mother had ordered before an instructor told me I was too "chunky" to continue lessons with her; a day when my friends and family all surrounded me—except for the one who had missed so many other days like this one; a day when "chunky" got all tangled up around "gone;" a day when I used my wish to say, *Let him come home.* Or maybe it was the twelfth one, when I stood on our front porch waiting for my whole invited class to show up and only a few did; a day when there was no call or note or card from the missing one; a day when there were no candles to wish upon, because I was too old or maybe she was too strapped; a day when I still made my wish on the first star in the sky: *I wish I could be pretty so he would come home.*

Or maybe it was the twenty-fifth one, when I had just quit a dream-come-true newspaper job to follow my husband on a church-planting adventure, a day when I decided I would spend my time writing, a day when I peed on a stick and it said yes, a day when I still made my wish on the candles my husband lined up on a cake he'd made himself: *I wish I could publish a book.*

Maybe it was all of them, because a tenth birthday came around, and he did not come home; and a thirteenth birthday came around, and my beauty, or lack of it, did not bring him home; and a twenty-sixth birthday came around, and I had not published a book.

Birthdays did not feel like friends at all, even to a nine-year-old girl. They felt like fingers pointing to all the ways I had disappointed time.

///

I wish I could say it's different this time around, but it's not. The day after my birthday this year, my job will end. It's the first time I have never worked for someone else. All that space feels more like an expectation, not a possibility. It's hard to explain, except by saying this: there is a birthday climbing on my back and whispering in my ear, *Another year older, and what have you done?*

The answer is *not much*, and so this birthday takes my words and cackles and throws all those other years, when wishes didn't come true, right back in my face. So when my husband asks if I want to celebrate with friends and family, I say no. Who wants to mark another year gone when there is nothing to show for it?

No published book, still. No job. Not even a family that is "put together" and "doing it" and functioning past the overwhelm that raises tempers and flings at each other words we don't really mean.

Only an aching back, because kids have pulled all the joints out of whack. Only anxiety that still claws at a neck, even though we're practicing meditation and exercising and learning to change our thoughts and I'm even popping a pill every day. Only a collection of dreams and wishes that never came true.

///

When I was eight years old I saw the movie *The Goonies* (still one of the best movies of all time), and I remember how, for days, I dreamt about all those skeletons. I would sit in the bathtub, and my mom would come check on me, and I would see a skeleton walking through the door. My little sister would be fast asleep in her bed when I came in, and I would see a skeleton lying between the pink sheet and the purple-striped blanket. I would imagine my dad, wherever he was in the world, slumped in a corner, in skeleton form, looking like One-Eyed-Willie, without the treasure waiting on a lost ship.

What I'd seen in a childhood movie had thrown reality at me, proven that one day we would all die, and one day we would all turn to skeletons like the ones Mikey and Bran and Mouth ran into. Death terrified me, because it looked like those brittle bones; sometimes it looked even scarier, like the wax figures lying in a casket. Neither one was what I wanted to be.

When I imagined getting older, I imagined death.

And just like that, a little girl broke off what should be

a happy relationship with her birthday. She didn't want to grow up. She didn't want to get any older. She didn't want to die.

///

So, you see, getting older has never been exactly easy for me. I was never the girl who couldn't wait until she turned ten or sixteen or twenty-one, because every one of those years felt like a step closer to death. And even this week, when another birthday has come and gone, it passed with more dread than excitement.

It's silly, when we get down to the heart of it, that we fear getting older. We, especially women, can feel time ticking so loudly—this many years until I can no longer have a baby, this many years until my hair turns all gray, this many years until they will no longer think of me as "young" and "beautiful."

What does it really matter?

There is a great gift in getting older, too, a wisdom that begins to settle into our bones when we realize that life is not really about these little things—having a job or not, publishing a book or not, making a name for ourselves or not. Life is really about who we become in all these years. Who we become in our families and in our communities and in our selves.

Will we become people who believe accomplishment and accolades and just-right circumstances tell the whole story of who we are? Or will we become people who believe that our true worth is really tied to who we were created to be, who we already are when we peel away all the layers a world can wrap us in?

We are all born with a diamond down deep inside us, and the diamond is brilliant and visible for a time, and then the world covers it in a great heap of armor, and then we spend the rest of our years trying to uncover it again so we can see and know and believe the treasure we already are, without the qualifications and accomplishments tagging behind our name. And if getting older means uncovering more of that brilliance, one shovelful at a time, then I want to embrace age. Wisdom. Maturity.

So this year, on my day, I didn't check for more gray hairs and moan about the wrinkles that have begun to gather around the corners of my eyes from smiling too much at my boys. I looked, instead, toward the gift that time holds out to me every single birthday: one more chunk of a diamond revealed.

And then I whispered my wish.

On Awards and Conformity

He's home from school now, this day when he was recognized by his teacher as Star Student, a lofty award, for his courtesy and help and kindness, and he hasn't stopped grinning since he walked through the door.

It's a badge of honor for this five-year-old boy who has watched friends accept the award and who wanted, desperately, to get it, too. And he did, and it's a victory of sorts, a validation in his little-boy mind, so much a part of him today that when we talk about a family movie night for Family Time and his brothers start throwing out suggestions, he puffs out his chest and says, *No! You don't get to pick because you weren't Star Student today.*

He's been doing it all afternoon, choosing what game they play together on the trampoline because he was Star Student, getting the biggest cookie because he was Star Student, asking to be excused from after-dinner chores because he was Star Student.

This time he looks at his daddy and me, as if we'll agree. We hardly know what to say. Hardly know what to do.

I feel the annoyance clogging the back of my throat, though, because who is he to think he is better or more privileged or more special than all of his brothers just because of some award? The annoyance almost hijacks my tongue, and then I remember that I was once him, too.

///

In elementary school, middle school, and high school, I lived for those awards, because they validated who I was. They made me forget my reality of fatherless, penniless girl and let me be someone important. Someone admired. Someone who could rise above.

My seventh grade year, when I'd been playing the clarinet for eighteen months, I played a scale for a chair test and missed a note. The boy who sat second chair played his scale perfectly while I sat in my seat, holding my breath, hoping, hoping, hoping he would miss two notes so he wouldn't knock me from the top spot I'd held all this time. The band director had us switch places, and I saw the whole world crumbling apart around me. Who was I now that I wasn't on top?

I cried hysterically in the bathroom all through that next class period. The world had ended for me in that moment. (It would begin again, of course. But to a twelve-year-old, it certainly felt like The End.)

It was the same with academics. I lived to be someone smarter, someone more talented, someone more important than my crowd of classmates, because I did not know then that I was great without one single accolade to prove it.

In high school every subject award went to me, because

I worked hard to stay first in my class, to stay "smartest." I believed I could lose my intelligence the same way I could lose an award. I lined up all the awards on my dresser at home, where I could see them every morning as I brushed my hair and put on makeup for school. So I could remember who I was.

I let those pieces of wood and brass tell me who I was, and I let them lock me in an iron cage that said I could not fail, ever. I could not let someone else collect an award, ever. Failure would tear my identity into tiny little, can't-put-back-together pieces.

I still have those awards, packed into a bin somewhere. They are rusting now.

///

Earlier this morning, before the award ceremony, my eight-year-old randomly said that in his more than two years of public school he has never been chosen a Star Student. Yesterday I'd gotten an e-mail from his kindergarten brother's teacher, saying the five-year-old had been chosen Star Student for this week. No one knew it yet except his daddy and me. Every Friday their elementary school has an assembly for the first twenty minutes of school time, where kids with birthdays and kids who have done something noteworthy and kids who are chosen Star Student are honored.

That morning my husband looked at me and then told our boy, *Maybe you can ask what you could do to be considered for the award*, but this answer doesn't feel quite right. What if the subjective requirements for an award like this one lie outside of who he is on the inside? We can't ask a kid to act outside of who he is, just to snag an award.

Ten minutes later, we watched our five-year-old beam while the announcer read what his teacher had written, how he can always be counted on to offer help, how he is almost always kind and courteous to his peers and adults, how he loves people and always looks forward to his lessons. And I can't help but feel proud, because this is exactly who he is, who he has always been: a boy skilled at interpersonal relationships and always looking for the places where he can help and encourage others.

But there is a shadow to this pride. I can't help but think of my eight-year-old, sitting with his second grade class, watching his little brother get an award he has never had the honor of receiving. Will he feel less than? Will he think he needs to be someone different? Will he believe that who he is is not good enough, because there is no award telling him any different?

And another questions chases these: Do awards do more good or more damage?

///

My second job out of college was working as a reporter for the *San Antonio Express-News*. Every day I'd crank out my stories, one after another, so I could help fill all those blank pages. I took care with all my words, because I wanted to get them right. I wanted to get them beautiful, too, especially for the feature stories. So I'd practice and revise and revise again, diligently perfecting every letter, every word, every turn of phrase before turning them in.

The Hearst Corporation, which owns the *Express-News* and a whole family of other reputable newspapers, would every quarter hand out awards for best news story or feature story or op-ed column or page design or photography. It was an award every reporter and designer and photographer coveted, not just because it came with a cash reward, but also because it came with bragging rights and admiration in the newsroom. Our editors would call a meeting on the second floor of the building, where all the news reporters worked, and I would walk with my colleagues in features down a flight of stairs, wondering who might win this time.

Winners were announced in front of the entire editorial staff.

I won two of them in my three years with the newspaper, and I could not have known how they would twist my confidence like a sadistic lover.

When I was winning awards, I was a *real* writer. When I wasn't, I was no writer at all.

Awards can do this ugly thing to us. They can make us forget all the really talented writers who join our ranks, who deserve those awards, too. We start thinking we can do it better than they can. We even start thinking we *need* to do it better than they can so we can win an award and prove our worth, because, we think, people will only know what we're worth with an award to back us up. We start thinking we might not have what it takes if we don't win.

It's an ugly place to be, waiting on a prize so you can know more surely who you are.

I didn't know it then, but I can see it now: those awards wrapped their pressure around me and whispered in a young-reporter ear, *You are nothing without our validation. Win or give up.*

///

I don't want this for my sons. I especially don't want it for the eight-year-old one, who may never get Star Student in his whole elementary career. He's a boy who has his own ideas about things. He's not afraid to question everything, and he's as strong-willed as they come. These aren't the traits that are typically awarded in a little boy. They aren't even encouraged.

For weeks I've listened to my five-year-old talk about wanting to win Star Student, because this is the pinnacle of success at their school, but is it the pinnacle of success for us, to be Star anything? I hope not. I hope, at the end of a day, I can say I am more interested in helping my boys stay true to who they are than I am interested in adding another award to the stack of to-keep memories from their school days.

Some Star Students are awarded for helping keep their

classroom clean and tidy. Some are awarded for their consistency in doing everything they're told the first time. Some are awarded for staying on task and never daydreaming about what they'll do as a filmmaker when they're grown.

But these are not the most important things in the world.

We reward kids for doing all the things that make our lives easier, but the world is sometimes better served by the kid who will stand up for what he believes in and challenge the status quo when it doesn't make sense anymore, even when it's inconvenient to us, the adults. If all we had in the world were perfect rule-followers, which is what awards like this tell us we need and should be, how would anything significant, like a civil rights movement or a "women deserve the right to vote" protest or save-the-environment programs ever happen? Of course it's easier and more convenient to be the parents of the kid who does everything he's asked to do, without question, who waits for instruction before starting a task (and completes it), who always has a kind, encouraging word to say, like my sweet five-year-old. I have a few of these in my house.

But there are times when I wish they would rebel like their oldest brother, because he is the one who shows me clearly where rules don't make much sense anymore. He is the one who always has those brilliant, out-of-the-box solutions. He is the one who will tell me when I'm being a complete ass (without the word, of course, only the very-accurate description). Who's to say which one is better and which one deserves an award? They both make me a better person.

My eight-year-old will try, for a time, to be the "model" Star Student, but he cannot deny who he is. And I'm so glad he can't.

His disappointment will open for us an opportunity to let him know that the people who take up the least space in a classroom or who demand the least amount of attention or who always do everything they're told the first time are not the only ones who can make a difference in the world. He will make a difference in this world, too, with his constant questioning and his creative mind and his rebellion.

This is who he is.

On Balance

I feel the annoyance creeping in, because it's the third time this morning I've tried to finish this sentence—just this one sentence—and the boys are fighting again, so the baby starts crying and then someone says those dreaded words: "I'm telling Mama."

It's unusual that I'm working right now while they're playing, but I sent some facts to be checked, and the source confirmed them late, and I have to finish this one little sentence, just seven words, to get it sent off before deadline. But a little boy is shaking my arm, trying to tattle on a brother who took his toy, and I drop my head and let out the longest sigh in the history of air and say, "Can you just let me finish this one little thing? It's such a little thing!"

He cries and blubbers and shakes my arm some more, so I shut the laptop harder than I intend to. I can feel all the wrong words exploding from my mouth.

Sometimes being a writer and a mother feels near impossible.

"I don't know how you get it all done and still have time to be a good mother," my friends and family occasionally say.

I understand the question, because mothering is hard and intense and never-ending. When in the world would I possibly have time to write? How does a good mother become a good writer? How does a good writer walk away from the writing desk still a good mother?

How does a woman change diapers and spend time with her children and kiss the booboos that happen every other minute and build a star out of shape blocks and still put coherent thoughts down on a page?

We become mothers and believe that's the end of our story.

But I want you to know it's not. Not if we don't want it to be.

///

When I was four years old, I could already read, mostly because my ten-months-older brother came home from kindergarten and taught me everything he learned that day in class.

Reading opened up a whole new world for me, and I loved it so much I wanted to contribute to it. So I sketched out my first stories, with characters called Laura and Mary and Carrie Ingalls. They would get into the same adventures my brother and sister and I would get into—meeting the ghost in the tree house out back, playing a risky game of dodge ball with the millions of pecans carpeting our backyard, building forts out of blackberry brambles before we knew they were mostly just ready-made snake nests.

I knew early on that I wanted to be a writer. I knew I wanted to write literature for children. I knew exactly what I had to do to get there.

I told everyone I knew of my plans. They agreed and nodded and patted me on the head with smiles that spoke of great amusement that here was a little five-year-old telling them what she wanted to be when she grew up, already, and watch how she would change those plans when she got older and real life happened.

Except the plans never changed. They didn't change when I went off to college and was encouraged by a guidance counselor to major in a field that would actually pay, so I picked journalism. I wrote out my fiction stories longhand in the extra hours between classes.

My plans didn't change when I married my husband and I got my first job at a large newspaper in Texas. I wrote my stories in the hours between dinner and sleep.

They didn't change when we had our first baby and started talking about the possibility of quitting our jobs and pursuing music together. This time, though, there was no time to turn plans into pursuit. So I put them on hold.

///

I didn't know they would be on hold for so long. I didn't know that my husband would quit his job and I would remain at mine, because it was flexible enough to allow travel and there was another baby on the way and someone had to have a steady paycheck so we could pay our bills and feed our growing family.

So I worked as a managing editor and took care of the baby and spent evenings practicing or playing gigs or trying to get some sleep even though there was so much, always, to do.

You couldn't really see it from the outside, but I was withering into only a piece of who I am. A piece doesn't live like a whole does. A piece has only a matter of time before it dies, cut off from the whole.

I was slowly dying, and no one could even tell.

///

Six years later I still felt stuck, working a job I hated, trying to make ends meet, trying to love kids well, trying to just keep up, trying to feel fulfilled. But all those stories were burning holes clean through me, and they kept getting deeper and wider and blacker.

I snapped at children and picked fights with my husband and became a person I didn't really like, because I felt so dried up inside. It didn't matter that I had all these beautiful boys or that my husband has only ever been supportive or that I got to work my job mostly from home so I had the best of both worlds—designing pages and editing articles while my kids romped around in the same room. It mattered that I wasn't writing. It mattered that I could not create all those stories that had lived in my imagination for more than a decade.

So I started taking moments where I could. When my boys were eating breakfast and we'd finished the morning devotional, I jotted down story ideas. When they napped, I crafted essays and chapters. When they went to bed at night, I wrote random thoughts in a nightly journal. When I read to them, I picked books that would make me a better writer. When we engaged in our after-dinner family time, we incorporated a writing time and independent drawing time for the littlest ones. When school let out for the summer, we brainstormed a family story-telling project.

Slowly, slowly, slowly, I started coming back to life.

///

It's never easy, being a mother who writes. I feel the pressure of do-it-all and try-to-look-perfect and volunteer-for-everything-at-my-kids'-school. I know many mothers who feel it, too.

We want to be the best mothers we can be. We want to have perfectly clean and put-together houses. We want to spend the most time we can in our kids' classrooms so the memories they have at school are always associated with us, too. We want to keep on top of laundry and cook the best and healthiest meals and organize an afternoon of pure fun for our children. Because we love them so much.

But we can't do it all. We can't. So we need to stop trying.

There's an easy answer to the question, "How do you do it all?" The truth is, I don't.

If you were to come to my house on any given day, you would see a thick layer of dust on the bookshelves, because I was busy building a flower garden out of shapes with my three-year-olds this morning and every other morning for the last three months. You would see the mess the four-year-old made with his crayons and art paper during his Quiet Time today, because he no longer naps and I needed to make deadline on an article. You would see that tonight we're having raw carrots and raw cucumbers tossed in a bowl, along with the chicken that's been simmering in the crockpot all day, because I had a lot on my mind that I needed to get down on paper.

You would see that the laundry has yet to be put away, even though I finished it three days ago. You would see that the six-year-old frequently bursts into my room when I'm in the middle of an essay and asks if I've seen the other Spider-Man sock that went missing. You would see that sometimes, when I'm sitting in my wing chair crafting a chapter on a novel, my eight-year-old will sneak quietly in and sit in his daddy's wing chair without saying a word for a whole hour, just because he wants to be near me.

This is what it looks like to be a working mom. It doesn't look perfect. It doesn't look neat all the time. It doesn't even look completely consistent, because sometimes someone throws up on the carpet and needs Mama to lie down beside him so his tummy feels better. Sometimes the twins won't stop fighting over who gets which train and Mama has to step in to defuse emotions. Sometimes the biggest boy threatens he's going to run away and I have to talk him out of it.

Some days all I can be is Mama. That's okay, too. Because do you know what living does? What engaging with our children does? What being a mama does? It makes our work richer.

Maybe we will always feel this tension between creating and mothering. Maybe we will always hear the voice that whispers we are being selfish in our pursuit and we should just be content with being a mother. Maybe we will always feel guilty that we want and need something more.

But what I have learned in my years being a writer *and* a mother is that I am a better wife and mother and person because of my creating.

This is whole-hearted living.

And it's way better than doing it all.

On Years and Changing

We're sitting in my living room, all our bellies full, and the twins are down for their naps while the oldest boys and the newest one are still up, hanging out with their Nonny and Poppy.

My mom holds the littlest one. My stepdad plays with the others. And somewhere in the middle of our conversation my mom says, "I sure never expected you to have six boys."

I laugh. "Yeah. Me neither," I say.

"If your high school friends could see you now," my mom says.

If they could, I thought. *They would not recognize this me I have become.*

I am not who I once was. Not even close.

And I am so very glad.

///

When I was twelve years old, I had just lost my dad to divorce. My mom was close to depressed. I lost my center.

I was never exactly popular, but I did have a handful of friends. And there was a best friend. We were inseparable. We stayed over at each other's houses—mostly hers, because I was ashamed of my beat-up one. I knew her sister and mother and father, and she knew my brother and sister and mother.

And then there came a day when jealousy flashed its ugly grin and I fell into its web. I don't know why, exactly. I just know that I was a fatherless child who was lost and alone and sad. Maybe that explains why it happened. Maybe it doesn't at all.

There isn't really a good excuse for being a mean girl.

It's just that I hurt so badly inside that the only way I felt like I could deal with my hurt was to hurt someone else. So she could feel what I was feeling. I was too young to understand that when you hurt someone else, you don't feel any less alone. You don't feel any better.

We were watching the eighth graders play a volleyball game. Our seventh grade team had just finished. For some reason I was sitting up high in the bleachers, and she was down at the bottom. Probably I had already said something mean, because we never sat separated from each other.

More mean was on its way.

A mutual friend moved between us. "Why don't you want to be her friend anymore?" she said when she reached the top of the stands.

"Because," I said, with my poker face on. "I just don't like her anymore."

Our friend walked back down the bleachers and relayed my message, because we were immature little girls using a mediator. I watched my best friend's face crumble, her heart breaking at the knowledge that I could just decide one day I didn't like her anymore. And why not? A daddy could decide he didn't like a little girl anymore and up and leave.

I spent five more years in the same school as my former best friend. Our friendship was never the same. I could not ever quite bear to look her in the eyes.

///

It's hard to say what changes us. Love. Children. Years. Life. All of these, rubbing at our edges and softening up the rough parts and uncovering the diamond of who we really are. We are born into the world pure and whole and beautiful, and then we start counting birthdays, and between those first days of life and now, the diamond of our identity starts disappearing little by little, covered by ego and pain and anxiety and fit in and popular and ridicule and normal, whatever that means.

Someone tells us we need to lose a little weight, and we forget that skinny does not equal beautiful. Someone tells us we need a thicker skin and we forget how big emotions can be a great gift. Someone tells us we aren't any good at something and we forget that opinions are just opinions and we don't have to be defined by them.

We forget that we are in charge of who we are and who we become, not "them." We can spend a whole lifetime trying to uncover that diamond again.

I look back at the girl I used to be, the girl who could

hurt a best friend with such irreverent, ugly words, and I am so glad I am no longer her but have become someone who is much more careful with words and the glass hearts of those I love. I look at the teenager who lashed out and tore down and felt diminished by another's success, and I am so glad I am no longer her. I look at the young woman who never wanted kids because she didn't want the changed body that came with them, and I am so glad I am no longer her.

///

I would do more over the years. I would hurt other friends. I would say things I didn't mean. I would try to make them feel what it felt like to live in my skin—rejected, ugly, unworthy. And then I would find myself on my knees in the middle of a concert hall, moved so deeply by the music that I could not even hold up my heaped-with-guilt head anymore. I could not look into the eyes of the ones there with me. I could only sob. And I would go back to my dorm and scratch out all my letters and dig through an address list of my old high school classmates, searching for the ones I needed. I would mail those letters off.

I would wait.

And the responses would come, one after another, telling of how touched they were that I had written and apologized, as if I could do anything else, and I would feel some small piece of healing bloom in my heart. And then, not long after that healing set in, the same thing would happen to me. A best friend would lash out. She would accuse and hurt and rip me clean apart.

And, God, it would hurt. But those places of forgiveness that others had extended to me would turn into places where I could forgive her, years later. Because, even then, I was not who I once was.

///

There is a wisdom that comes with love and children and years and life, but we can miss it. We can miss it because we are bent beneath the weight of guilt for all those things we did before. We can miss it because we are listening to who "they" say we should be. We can miss it because we are walking broken and we are walking breaking, like wrecking balls crumbling anything they touch.

The years twist some of us into smaller versions of ourselves, because they march on hard and violent and unfair. But the good news is, we get to stamp The End to that victim story. We get to choose to become someone better.

We can heap more dirt on top of our diamond or we can uncover more of its brilliance. It's entirely up to us.

It's not ever easy leaning into our transformation. It's not ever comfortable rounding off our edges and cutting out the pieces that no longer belong, but where we end up will be worth all that pain. We will be someone greater, someone truer to ourselves, someone who knows what it's like to be on the wounded side and the wounding side and has lived to tell about it.

    The world can't help but be changed by our changing. I am not who I once was. And I am so very glad.

On Overcoming Criticism

This whole afternoon, since getting home from school, he's been quiet and withdrawn, and I know him well enough to know that there is something weighing heavily on his eight-year-old heart. So even though I should be working and he's caught me in the middle of a story, I set my laptop on the coffee table and turn my full attention to him.

"What's bothering you, baby?" I say.

Sometimes he talks and sometimes he doesn't, so I'm not entirely prepared for what he says: "Some kids were mean to me at school today."

And the first thing I want to know is who, because being mean to my boy is not tolerated in my mama heart. It takes great effort to ask a different question instead.

"Oh, yeah?" I say. "What happened?"

He was playing on the playground today, he says, and he asked his friends if they might want to play a Power Buddies game he'd made up. Power Buddies are characters my boy has been developing for a year now, superheroes with elemental super powers. He has created a whole new world where they exist and loves to share that imaginary world with his friends. Often, they play along willingly.

"They said Power Buddies were stupid," he says, and his voice breaks clear down the middle. "They said I would never write their stories and publish them in a book. And even if I did, no one would read them."

He's crying hard now because of this hurt. Blood starts roaring in my ears.

I have been here before, too.

But I don't try to fix it. I don't try to make him feel better. I just fold my boy in my arms and let him cry at this hurt from friends he thought loved him the way he loves them.

There will be time for what comes next.

///

My second year of college I signed up for an introductory creative writing class. The first day of class I knew I wouldn't like my professor. He was arrogant and overly opinionated and rigid in his beliefs about the one way things should be done. I've never much liked arrogant, overly opinionated, and rigid people.

The first poem I turned in was a religious one about how dark and light can coexist. It wasn't very good, but it wasn't bad enough to merit the big red C he marked on it. He'd scrawled a piece of explanation across the back page. "Leave religion out of class," it said. So I did. And yet every poem I turned in after that he marked "melodramatic" or "flowery" or "fluff," no matter how happy or dark or serious I got. He used my short stories as material to rip apart in class, in front of the twenty or so other students.

He was a bully through and through, set on discounting me at every turn. But I didn't drop the class, because I was not a quitter. I stuck around and kept trying, kept getting better. He never could bring himself to acknowledge that I was the hardest worker in the class.

When he handed back my last short story of the semester, it was with discouraging words. I forget what they were, exactly, but they were something along the lines of, "You will never be published. Look for something else to do. Your writing is not good enough."

The words dropped down deep and sat there like permanent stones.

///

If we're not careful, the words that others speak so carelessly can become more than just words. They can become lies that we believe.

I let those words of my first creative writing professor derail me for a while. I let them tell me what I could and could not do. I let them still my pen, because, of course, he was right. What was the point?

For six years, every time I tried to pick up a pen, his voice came whispering from that dark wound in my heart.

No one cares about this story, he said.

These characters are boring, he said.

You will never, he said.

We Count it All Joy

And then, one day, I decided to test that lie. I decided to open my notebook. I decided to write.

The thing about those critical voices is that when we test them and find them as untrue as they actually are, they then have the potential to launch us into greater determination and effort. I let the words wreck me for a time. I gave up, but my giving up didn't make me feel any better. I knew what I was made to do, and letting someone else determine whether or not I did it left me hollow and shaky on the inside.

So I chose to write—not to prove him wrong but to prove to myself that I could do it when someone said I couldn't.

Sometimes those voices aren't curses. Sometimes they are the greatest blessings of all—because in overcoming them, we learn how surprisingly resilient we are.

///

Two years ago I sat in the lobby of a hospital with my husband for a meeting with the pastor of a large church where my husband was spending a few months as the interim worship pastor. The pastor had called a meeting to tell us that if we were to move forward, if my husband was to get the worship pastor job, I would have to stop leading worship with him.

My voice simply wasn't good enough for the size church he led, he said.

I was playing in the big leagues now, and I didn't have

what it took to compete, he said.

There would be no husband-and-wife music ministry at *his* church, he said.

I sat and listened to his words, and I would not let the crumbling inside make me cry. I didn't say a single word about his thoughts, just thanked him for his time and walked numbly back to the car with my husband when the torturous meeting had finished.

I spent a whole year reeling. My husband and I found somewhere else to serve, where people made it their mission to seek us out after the service ended and tell us how much they enjoyed our voices together. They couldn't see it from where they sat, but every single time I got up to the microphone to sing—every single time—I heard that pastor's voice.

Not good enough, he said.

I believed him. I believed him even though my husband and I had been in a band for a decade and had three full-length albums under an independent record label. What if all of it was actually really bad, because of me? I couldn't bear the thought. So I stopped writing music. I stopped singing. I stopped offering our worship leading services to the people with whom I came in contact, because they wouldn't want us anyway.

And then, months later, I stood up, and there was a big, gaping hole where the music had been. So I started crawling back to it, writing a song here and there, tentatively at first. I started singing in the hallways of our home so my kids would smile at my silly lyrics that they hadn't heard in too long.

I started to call that pastor's voice a lie.

///

Sometimes those words can hit us so hard we don't think we'll ever get back up. Sometimes it takes us a really long time to get back up. Six months. A year. Six years.

It's hard to say what makes people use their voices this way. Sometimes they're jealous. Sometimes they're just set on their own way and don't care if getting that way is cruel. Sometimes they don't understand the responsibility that comes with their speech-freedom. It doesn't really matter why, really. What matters more is what we do with their words. Will we let them define a new, broken us? Or will we let them propel us into a new, better us?

Even though those voices shout loud and hit hard at all our weakest places, we don't have to bend. We don't have to break. We don't have to let the stones inside. We can let them drive us deeper into the journey of discovering who we are and what we can do, because we know, deep down, why we are here and who we are becoming and what we must do.

We know whether or not those voices and their words are true, and it doesn't matter if they feel true in this moment right here, right now. It only matters that we call them FALSE.

Who would I be without writing? Who would I be without music? Fulfilled? Satisfied? Happy?

No.

Then I must keep on. No matter how many voices gather against me, no matter what those voices say, no matter how loud they get.

My boy has finished his grieving. I pull back only when several minutes pass without a sniff.

"Do you think your friends are right?" I say.

He shrugs. "I don't know."

"Do you think you would be happy if you didn't write your Power Buddy stories?" I say.

"No," he says. We look in each other's eyes. "I want to tell their stories."

"Then what are you going to do?" I say.

He's quiet for a minute, and then he says, "I'm going to write their stories. Will you help me, Mama?"

Of course I will. Of course I will help my son prove to himself that he can do something others say he can't. Because I want him to know that "they" can't tell us who we are or what we can or cannot do. "They" are not us. "They" have no idea why we have been put here. But we do.

So every Wednesday night, during our snuggle time, we have been brainstorming a brand new Power Buddy series. We are telling those stories together, my son and me.

Even though people said he couldn't.

We Count it All Joy

Even though people said it was stupid.
Even though people said no one would read them.
We do it anyway. Because we know.
This is wholehearted living.

On Success

We're sitting around the table, talking about our days like we always do, when my husband says, "We got some negative podcast feedback today."

"Oh, yeah?" I say.

He tells me about this product manager with Facebook, who wrote in to say that as much as he wants to recommend the show to his friends, he just can't do it because of my husband's involvement. My husband, according to this man, hasn't had the kind of success people would expect from a business owner giving business advice.

This exchange comes at the beginning of our meal, just before we get to our thankfuls, and it thoroughly and completely derails me. So it gets to my turn, and I can barely think of anything that deserves my thanks, my whole mood shot through with rips and holes and great big tears. I think about my lost job and our money worries and what might or might not come next in the lineup of success, and my stomach twists, way deep down.

My husband knows, of course, because he's that kind of man. He smiles and says, "It doesn't really matter. I know I'm successful." And I know he's right and I know he knows, but something about it just won't let me go.

That word, success, is a dirty one, snaking all through my past.

A man's hasty criticism sends it striking again.

///

I spent my four years of high school constantly stressed about grades—because, you see, I wanted to go to college, and I knew my mom and stepdad could not afford it. I needed to graduate valedictorian, because it was the only way I would make it to college, since valedictorians in Texas are given free tuition at their college of choice for at least the first year of attendance. So I watched those class rankings, every six weeks, like they were life and death.

I came out on top, and my classmates held an election right before graduation for all the yearly yearbook awards: Most Beautiful, Most Talented, Most Athletic, Most Popular. They voted me Most Likely to Succeed.

"Because you're smart," they said. "Because you know so much. Because you always find a way."

They could never have known the pressure that award carried in its flimsy paper particles and its forever photo buried in a maroon yearbook.

I went off to college, one hundred twenty-six miles from home. I had never been away from home longer than three weeks at a time, and by month two, I wanted so very badly to go home I cried myself to sleep every night. I missed my mom. I missed my whole family. I missed all the familiar. But I could not go back, because that is not something a person who was Most Likely to Succeed would do.

So, on the worst nights, I pulled out the coloring page my fifteen-year-old sister had sent me, the one with Garfield and Odie colored in muted oranges and yellows, the one that said, "Wish you were here" in a little cloud bubble beside Garfield's scowling face. And I whispered what I could never, ever admit to anyone.

I do, too.

///

Success comes breathing down our necks, and its breath is foul and suffocating and inescapable—because it is everywhere in the world. In magazines profiling the "most successful" people in the world, according to how much they're worth in a year's salary. On billboards where famous personalities tell us to watch their shows. In books and on screens and next door to us, where the Joneses live.

Success looks like how big a business you build in the least amount of time or how much money you have in your bank account. It looks like big houses and luxury cars and a name that means something when spoken.

Success, the way the world defines it, carries pressure in its scales. It can hypnotize us into believing its shallow lies. It will tell us what to do and how to live and who we should be.

I can see its venom weaving in and out of all my

younger years. I took jobs and turned others away because of it. I bought a two-door silver five-speed car because of it (two doors looks more successful than four, silver is sleeker than blue, five-speed is faster than automatic). I wanted a bigger ring because of it (because the bigger the diamond, the greater the catch, right?). I fell hard into its nest.

And then something happened.

///

As college graduation approached, I did not worry like all my friends. I already had a job at the *Houston Chronicle*. I had a brand new car and thousands in the bank. I had an engagement ring on my finger.

I was going to be prolific.

For a time, that Most Likely to Succeed award felt just right. I was proving it true.

Money? Check.

Prestigious job? Check.

Husband? Check.

By the end of that year, I would add several writing awards to the list, and later we would start a band and play around town and then the state and then all the way up through the Midwest.

On the road home from a gig in New Mexico, my cell phone rang. It was my mother. My grandmother, she said, was dead.

My grandmother, the one I'd lived with for a year

during my childhood, when my parents were divorcing. My grandmother, who had offered her house for six months during that *Houston Chronicle* job and cried the day I left for San Antonio's newspaper. My grandmother, beside whom I was too busy to sit those nights she watched the news—instead holing away in a room planning my elaborate Cinderella wedding.

Her death devastated me. I counted back all those married months, forty of them, and I had only seen her three times—once after we returned from our honeymoon and she picked us up from the airport and begged us to stay the night, because it was too late to drive from Houston back to San Antonio and she knew we were tired from the flight, and we said no, because we wanted to get home and get on with our married lives; once for our year anniversary trip to Disney World, when we needed her to drop us by the airport; once when she came down for my firstborn's baby dedication, the day I watched her hold him from the stage while I cried through singing the lullaby I'd written for him.

How had this happened?

My grandmother was a school accountant of some kind for all her working life. She never made much money, never kept any money in savings because she was too busy buying her grandkids gas so they'd drive to see her or treating her kids to dinner or writing a check for a granddaughter's wedding dress. She stayed put in a no-promotions job because she enjoyed the summers off and the way she could keep her grandkids for whole weeks at a time.

I learned something the day we all gathered to celebrate her life. I learned, or maybe I always knew, that she was the very definition of success.

///

Success lives in who we are, not what we have.

Success is found in the way we look at our spouse in the middle of an argument. It's found in the way we talk to our children when they've done something wrong. It's found in the relationships we keep with family and friends and neighbors and strangers. It's found in the deepest spaces of a heart. The world, the ignorant words of others, the critical eyes of people, can make us forget this.

Sometimes people will look at our choices—having and raising six children, turning down a promotion because it would take too much time away from those children, remaining a one-car family because we don't want the debt—and stamp us unsuccessful because we don't look like the ideal. But success can never be measured on the outside. It is held within.

I wish I had realized that sooner in my life. I will never get back the time I spent pursuing a twisted version of success.

But I can redeem it now.

So tonight, in front of my boys who will one day be

men with a whole world and its people trying to tell them what success means, I look my husband in the eye and say, "You are successful in all the ways that matter."

And then I tick them off, all those successful attributes so much a part of who he is.

We may not have a bank full of money we couldn't spend in a lifetime or two luxury cars sitting out front or a vacation home in that place we always wanted to live. But what we do have, this life full of laughter and presence and joy, is so much better than all that.

The world can take its success definition and cash it in for an empty life.

I'll take my full one any day.

Visit www.racheltoalson.com for more of Rachel's books.

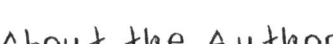

About the Author

Rachel has been practicing the fine art of essay writing for more than a decade. She is the kind of reader who enjoys reading the thoughts and philosophies of others, however they may differ from her own, because she believes that we all have significant contributions to make in the lives of others.

When she is not buried in the pages of a new essay collection, Rachel enjoys writing poetry and fiction for adults, young adults, and kids. She is the author of *The Colors of the Rain*, a middle grade novel-in-verse, three humor essay books, two poetry books, and nine middle grade fantasy books under a pen name.

She lives with her husband of fourteen years and her six sons in San Antonio, Texas.

www.racheltoalson.com

A Note from Rachel

Dear Reader,

If you are reading this note, I applaud both your curiosity and your generosity. I'm the kind of person who reads author's notes, but I suspect most readers skip right over them. Thank you for sticking around.

I hope that in the reading of this book you have felt our thread of shared humanity. I hope that you have felt less alone in your day-to-day movement through this hard but spectacular life. I hope you have found yourself and the joy with which every trial can be, if not welcomed or embraced, at least reframed. I hope my words will live on in you.

If you find yourself wondering how you might be able to get this book into the hands of others, I have two simple suggestions.

1. Share it with your friends. An author has no greater ally than word of mouth. Book recommendations from other readers is a great way to improve a book's likelihood of reaching the people who most need it.

2. Leave a review. Reviews help book buyers decide whether or not this book is for them, thereby, once again, getting it into the right hands.

I appreciate every effort you make to tell others about my work. Be sure to stop by www.racheltoalson.com and say hello.

You matter. You are loved. Don't ever forget this.

In love,

Rachel

Acknowledgments

This book took years of perfecting and shaping. It would not have been possible without:

My husband: Thank you for helping me find the courage to speak my truth and for loving me in spite of my often-mysterious feelings.

My family: Thank you for being so accommodating about your appearance in this book (and if you didn't know: Sorry).

My sons: Thank you for being exactly who I needed. You've made me who I am.

My blog readers: Thank you for providing such positive feedback, for sharing, for embracing my faltering heart and calling it, still, beautiful.

Reader Library

Speak to Me of Life is a collection of short essays on love, children, identity, anxiety, and creativity, among many other topics. But mostly it is a book about life—life lived to its fullest. Life lived in love, freedom, and joy. Life lived without fear.

Rachel takes her readers on a trip through the inner terrain of a heart, stopping only to say, in conclusion: Don't be afraid to be you.

Get *Speak to Me of Life* FREE for a limited time:

Visit* racheltoalson.com/freebook

*Must be 13 or older to be eligible

Enjoy more titles from Rachel Toalson

 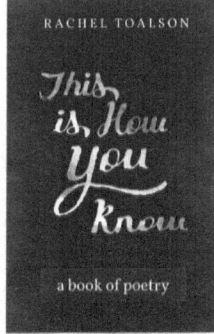 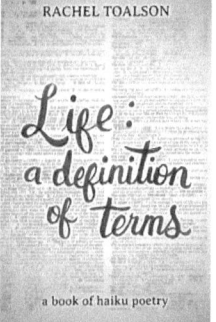

racheltoalson.com

www.ingramcontent.com/pod-product-compliance
Lightning Source LLC
Chambersburg PA
CBHW021428080526
44588CB00009B/464